Peaceful Meridian:
Sailing into War,
Protesting at Home

Aug 2020

Peaceful Meridian: Sailing into War, Protesting at Home

David Rogers Jr.

atmosphere press

To my father
The first sailor I knew

In this year of riots I am called to duty
Through this year of angers I have gripped a meaning
In this year of lies and angers burning out of control I went
    out and met history on its own terms
And I have come back to tell you what I saw:

    —Charles Upton, *Panic Grass*

WAR

Entrance

Everyone waits in the USO at O'Hare airport. Dozens and dozens, watching crap TV, some talking in whispers, some just sitting and thinking. It is not said, but it is implied that you cannot leave. Over the hours more show up from all over the country, flying to gather at this singular point— a trap of their own choosing. The room fills until there is no place to sit and even the floor is covered with recruits taking their last few moments of rest before boot camp. The sun goes down. Eventually the word is given to line up and go to the waiting bus that takes us to Great Lakes Naval Training Center.

It was strange being in Chicago this way. The suburban skyline along I-94 was my skyline. My eyes locked into it for the comfort found in familiarity, mentally tracing the outlines of buildings I had driven past my entire life. The names of the suburbs streaking by on exit signs were as familiar as the rooms in the family home: Rosemont, Des Plaines, Wheeling, Northbrook. These were places where my friends had lived, where we hung out or spent all night driving, talking, and getting into the minor sorts of trouble that kids used to figure out who they were or wanted to be. All was out of reach behind the glass of the bus window. Passing through like this, on a bus with strangers, felt like hearing someone you don't know describing your life back to you. Everyone else on the bus was in an alien city; I was both home and not home at the same time. My journey away from Illinois had failed and the Navy brought me back, slinking in personal defeat. I did not want the city to look back at me and see my ignominy.

As soon as the bus pulled through the gates of Great Lakes Naval Training Center my civilian life ended. We were mustered out of the bus and lined up under bright warehouse lights. Next, we were given a basic set of Navylogo sweats and bone-white gym shoes to wear. All my personal belongings and civilian clothes went into a box to be shipped away. Some loved one would, in a few days, receive a cardboard urn of my previous self. There was a chance to make one phone call; of course, the phone didn't work. More lines and gear issue. Drug tests were implemented to quickly weed out the indulgers on the previous night's send-off by friends and family and lovers. Eventually, through some arcane process I was divided out of the crowd of hundreds of new recruits and assigned to a division, a group of about 60. We were marched off to our barracks to spend our first night in boot camp sleeplessly. I am certain I was not the only recruit staring off into the dark. For nine weeks we were to be locked into the isolation of the training center, a military island of indoctrination amidst the urbanity of the Chicago suburbs. Seamanship on a concrete-locked ship.

I lay that night wondering at the abstract unreality of the day. It seemed like it had happened to someone else. And I also wondered, how did I get here? Why did I do this to myself?

Reasons

I joined because I was bored.

Some people can be happy in a standard job and a standard life. They attain those things and stop growing. There's no voice that picks away in those moments before and after sleep. For others, the voice wants something different, something adventurous, and it can only be ignored for so long. Then it resurfaces as depression, or an explosive temper, or a burning wistfulness. The urge to do something new, something different, something that breaks everything that happened before, becomes overwhelming.

That voice was one I heard every waking moment. One day, while waiting to board an airplane to somewhere in an attempt to relieve my boredom, I was reading a book about the Battle of Jutland, the massive naval battle in the North Sea during World War One. On the morning of the battle the crews were given a heartier breakfast than usual, large enough to get them through the upcoming fight. In a few hours many of those sailors would be wounded or dead. I wondered what it would have been like to sit on that mess deck and look around, not knowing who would survive the next few hours and who would not. Or would it be you torn in half by a German shell, or drowned in a flooding compartment in the cold dark? By trying to put myself in the minds of those sailors, I saw an experience far more vibrant and crucial than the small life I had, even if their experience was one of deprivation, hardship and violence.

Being broke had a good bit to do with the decision to join the military, as well. When I enlisted, I was living in Lincoln, Nebraska and had recently been laid off from my job. The small tech start-up had run out of money, as start-ups tend to do, and there was not a multitude of tech-oriented employers to choose from in such a small city. I did get a new job, but it was chosen out of necessity and not career advancement or passion. It was a job, nothing more, going nowhere and signifying nothing to me. I tried to make it work; tried the lie of saying that this is what I wanted, and passion was for fools and artists. As a Midwesterner it was pounded into me that adventures were for rich people and delusional idiots, and the best thing to do would be to take the first job I could get, stay in it for the rest of my life, and watch TV instead.

I had read too many books and had too active an imagination for that, but that model of life still held a powerful sway over me, enough to keep me from taking the leap into the dark I really needed. It's true, instead of joining the military, I could have just moved somewhere else and started a new life. I had a cousin in Colorado. Every time I visited her the mountains called to me. But pulling up stakes and moving West invited risk, and a Midwesterner is nothing if not risk averse. The military could provide an adventure with a paycheck and benefits. Ironically, the military, which is inherently physically dangerous, was the safest bet, financially and in predictability. When I reached the point in life when I did not know what to do with myself, it made a certain sense to turn to the military. Financial need in combination with existential boredom made military service an appealing choice.

And it had to be the Navy. Family tradition decreed as such. My maternal grandfather, John Nickley, served in the Merchant Marine during World War Two. My father David Sr. and his brother, Frank Rogers, served in the Navy during the Cold War. There was no doubt that, when choosing a service, it had to be one that went to sea.

Those are my reasons. Everyone who joins has some unique complex of emotions, rational thought and perceived necessity that makes them sign up at the recruiting station. Some join because they're broke. Many, to escape from a life they can't stand and didn't want. Some escape into a new life, seeing nothing ahead of them for all the years they have to live. Others join because they love their country. A few, a very few, just love the military life. One thing about being in the military, everyone you meet has a story. It is always a unique story, and often not a happy one. Happy people do not join the military.

Boot Camp

Boot camp is nine weeks, if you don't get sick and don't screw up. I entered in mid-January of 2004. It was, unfortunately, a record winter in Chicago and the nine weeks were dark, cold and snow-covered.

My division, number 115, was led by a chief petty officer and two assistants of lower rank, first class petty officers. The division was all male. There were a few mixed male and female divisions in boot camp, who trained together but slept in separate compartments. Our compartment (we used ship terminology for the buildings so a room was a compartment, a floor was a deck, and so on) was in an old building, dating back to who-knew-when in naval history. The bulkheads were painted cinderblock and the deck bare concrete. The space was long and narrow with two rows of bunkbeds, one down either side of the compartment. Windows were high up and longer horizontally than vertically, with worn brass fittings and frosted glass. They opened just enough to let some air in but not wide enough for a recruit to crawl out and make a run for freedom, if boot camp proved to be too much for them.

Chief was a shortish, compact and muscular man, dark-haired, with a vicious squint but mild outward mannerisms. We only saw him lose his temper once, when he kicked over a table at some recruit infraction and ranted about the family sacrifice he had made for his career. Bitterness and disappointment lurked close to the surface of that authoritative manner, barely kept in check by a love of the Navy and pride in service. Chief had just finished pushing through an excellent division, one who he said gave him no trouble and "just got it." He expected us to do just as well. He gave us a speech meant to reassure us that if we just paid attention and helped each other, boot camp could be easy. "Easy day" was one of his favorite phrases. It was his intention to turn us into an antidote to the bad and lazy sailors he had seen out in the fleet, to send us out like a cure for cancer. Every night he read to us, as we lay in our racks, a different story about a sailor who had won a Medal of Honor to instill the standard he wanted us to live up to.

Initially, boot camp is all about medical examinations and immunizations. Fortunately, those drop off relatively quickly after the first couple weeks. The exams are embarrassingly thorough. The worst for me was the inoculations. I'm terrified of needles. I was a sickly child and so had way too many shots when I was too young to understand why and learned to fear them. But since in the military you can go anywhere in the world at a moment's notice and face any natural disease and a host of biological weapons, you get lots of shots. Not only in boot camp but throughout your military career. Maybe it was the numbness of the first week in boot camp, but I was surprised when I did not pass out during the inoculations. Or perhaps it was the speed of the shots, as you run the gauntlet of medics with air-powered needle guns hitting you on both sides. I just didn't have time to be scared. And fortunately, that cured my fear of shots to this day. I still can't do blood draws, though. I pass out every time.

There also was a training film on the horrors of venereal disease. The less said of that gruesome spectacle, the better.

Being around each other all day every day, the recruits of Division 115 started to get to know one another. Everyone in the division was odd in their own way. Simply joining the military was a statement that you were a misfit who did not fit in with the American Dream. You had decided to eschew the bachelor's degree and mortgage, or the blue-collar job and trade school. Or you had just had bad luck that put those things out of reach. A lot of kids were just directionless, but at least were self-aware enough to know that they had to do something, and the military was an accessible way to a steady life. A few eager hard-working quiet recruits had to be let go because of failed background checks or drug tests. Nobody criticized them when they were gone. There was a young, idealistic virgin who didn't get picked on but instead garnered sympathy. There were surprising kindnesses as only found among the rejected.

I wasn't the only "old man" in Division 115. My rack mate in boot camp was Jon Hutto, a fellow thirty-something. He immediately stuck out as a non-conformist in the division. The day he shaved his epic beard was one of the highlights of the first two days of boot camp. Chief put us together as he thought it would be good to have the two old guys keep an eye on each other. We did that and talked often about politics and philosophy, and I found a fellow political progressive in the middle of the most regressive place I had ever been. Jon Hutto and I shared the same ability to keep our mind and soul separate from the training. He took keen interest in my stories of growing up around the women's movement in the 1970s and going to political events with my mother. Jon had a bachelor's degree, as did I, so our view of the world was different from the teenagers we were surrounded by. We were both liberal in our ideals but lost as well, looking for stability and self-expression that we could not connect with yet inside ourselves.

On occasion, an inspection was performed where we had to stand at attention next to our racks. A visiting Chief would walk down the line and quiz us about military matters. Sometimes, to throw people off, the Chief would ask the next recruit in line whether the previous answer was correct or not. Often the recruit would get flustered and automatically answer "no" even when the answer was correct.

Hutto was quizzed about some piece of naval trivia. His answer, shouted in the official format "Chief yes Chief!" was absolutely correct.

I, next in line, was asked to either correct his answer or confirm it. "Chief, he is correct, Chief!" I answered. "Yes, he was!" yelled Chief and walked down the line to the next victim.

Jon never forgot that I had his back in that moment and it led to further friendship later out in the fleet, and an interesting and vital political project.

After the initial shock wears off and boot camp becomes a daily routine, the day revolves around two main events; exercise and food. Getting in shape was good for me. I have always been a good runner, and had practiced before I left home, so getting back up to speed was not a problem. Calisthenics and muscle gain was more difficult. Most of the recruits were nowhere near military physical shape and the first evaluation ended badly, one of the few times our Chief fully let his anger loose. He made it known that we were going to be worked extra hard to make our next evaluation.

He got in the habit of stalking the mess hall table to see who had grabbed a dessert and pushed back their weight loss progress. He couldn't stop us; it was a rule that everything on the mess line was fair game and a recruit could eat as much as they wanted to, even if that meant the informal wrath of their Chief. Besides, Cake Man was singing. Cake Man was a civilian worker in the mess line who manned the dessert section at the end. He sang the wonders of cake loudly across the mess hall every day while we queued with our trays and gave recruits something to smile about in the harshness of boot camp.

Fortunately, my lack of a sweet tooth helped me avoid

Chief's anger but hearing Cake Man was a highlight of my dreary day anyway, a reminder of the real life outside the boundaries of boot camp. Here was a man who was happy enough to sing and got to go home every day. I would sing too.

Along with physical training at the gym we also were instructed in all the arts and skills of being a sailor. This included things like mooring and unmooring ships, nautical terminology, chain of command, and damage control. Much as every Marine is a rifleman, every sailor is a firefighter. We had to learn how to work a firehouse, patch a hole in a ship, fix a gushing pipe, and wear breathing apparatus in smoke-filled air. Much of this training took place on a small mock ship that had been built in a hangar, about the size of a tugboat. It had all the accoutrements of a real ship, ropes and bollards and a bell and ship's whistle and hatches and whatnot. It was actually rather impressive, sort of the ultimate sailor's playground. It was a shame we did not have any unstructured time to simply run around and play pirates.

Along with all the naval training, we were also taught more prosaic skills such as sewing a button or ironing a shirt. I went through these sessions with bemusement, since I already knew those basic life skills. But it was interesting watching the other recruits' reactions. There were half-hearted attempts at dismissive manliness among a few. Our chief petty officer made the point that these weren't effeminate skills, they were basic knowledge for everyone.

Along with the hands-on instruction we also had classroom training. This entailed listening to a lecture about navy history or the chain of command or nautical terminology. None of this was difficult except for the challenge of staying awake in too-warm classrooms. Still, some of the things we were taught were a shock. There was a class that ostensibly was about history but was actually anti-terrorism indoctrination. The instructor, a civilian, went on about the Tamil Tiger rebellion in Sri Lanka, and fumed against the adage "one man's terrorist is another man's freedom fighter." The Tigers were obviously terrorists and should get no one's sympathy, he stated. It struck me as strange that an American could have such a strong opinion about a conflict on the other side of the world in a country most Americans never heard of, a conflict with no threat to the United States or American interests at all. It was simply a civil war, a terrible one, but a war with no connection to us at all. Why would this instructor have such a strong opinion of something he didn't understand?

I came to realize that this was part of the general post-9/11 fear of Islam. Any political action by any Muslims in any country was a threat to the West. The only way to counter this threat was to obey the law and leaders and do what we were told. This went for civilian Americans as well as for the military.

We also got gassed. To give us confidence in our gas masks we had to march into a gas chamber, which was then filled with tear gas. Taking off our masks into the gas we had to recite part of the sailor's creed to make sure we got a good lungful of gas before being allowed to leave. The whole experience was absurd. It had nothing to do with gas mask confidence. This test, coming towards the end of boot camp, was a test of obedience. The purpose was to determine whether we were ready to obey any order no matter how dangerous, uncomfortable or foolish.

The strangest experience for me though was shooting a gun. In boot camp you do basic pistol training. My family is very Chicago middle class, so we're not a gun family. No one in the family owned one and no one saw a need to. They were considered unnecessary and socially and politically gauche; an indication of irrational fear and empty masculinity. I had never shot a gun before. On gun range day I wasn't exactly nervous but I wasn't excited either.

Shooting a gun proved to be very anti-climactic. We all lined up in our individual shooting booths, hearing protection on. The pistol was already there in front of me on the shelf. We listened to the instructions carefully. Trainers walked behind us, guns on their hips in case anyone took this opportunity for revenge or anger management issues.

The gun was heavy in the hand. It was just a tool, cold and blunt. It wasn't intimidating but the responsibility demanded bland focus. I shot my rounds, reloaded when told to, shot again. I felt no sense of power or masculinity. The shooting range became a day like any other.

The marching was incessant. Everywhere we went we marched in formation in perfect step, our place in the formation never changing. Being in sync with the rest of the division was required, and one recruit was tasked with a very simple sing-song to keep our pace correct and our feet coordinated. Very shortly it was second nature and done without thought. The goal, along with military smartness, was to inculcate us with a subconscious ability to work together and act as a unit. One evening on the parade group our chief had the vocal cadence stopped. He wanted to see how synchronized the division was, whether we would stay in step or drop off as soon as the cadence stopped. We marched in the dark silently, every step coordinated perfectly, eerily. Our Chief, a submariner, told us to be quiet and stealthy, just like the silent service.

All the marching also was leading to the graduating ceremony. I was chosen to be one of the flag bearers for the graduation, which meant learning the proper way to handle and carry the flagpole and coordinating each move with the music and spoken sections of the graduation. It was an extra little honor and led to some pleasant moments where those of us who were part of the honor guard could break away on our own to an unused compartment in the barracks and practice. It was the only time we were out of sight of authority and while we practiced sincerely we also relaxed, practically the only time we could.

Being already 30 years old, I had learned the skill of simply knuckling down, watching what was happening, and adjusting accordingly. Good workplace skills translated into good boot camp survival skills. Every day simply became a grind from waking up to going to sleep. In that way, the military and middle-class life were basically the same.

Being an older introvert helped in boot camp. Shielding myself from outside influences was already a habit. Every moment I was still myself, even if on the outside it appeared that my obedience was natural. Unlike many of my fellow recruits, I had read the news and knew my history so the indoctrination was not going to take hold.

Despite my improving health I still got sick and injured. The first challenge was marching in the record-setting snow in Chicago that winter. After several weeks my Achilles tendons ached. The constantly pushing off against the snow at every step took its toll. I powered through without complaint, just wanting to get to the end.

A bigger issue was a bad flu. One evening in the division compartment I felt nauseous. I ran to the bathroom to throw up. I vaguely heard someone telling Chief that I was sick. Skeptically, he entered the bathroom as I was vomiting in a stall (faking illness to get easy duty is a centuries-old sailor trick, called "malingering"). I heard him say, "oh, you really are sick." Next day I was at sick call in the central medical clinic.

I was diagnosed with a cold and given a day of bedrest.

While everyone marched off to class and the gym and other training I was allowed to sleep and recover. It was a blissfully quiet day with only a couple other sick recruits in the compartment. I remember the warm softness of the sunlight through the frosted glass of the ancient windows as I moved in and out of deep sleep. Later, after boot camp, as a vague abdominal pain would return on occasion accompanied by a bad cold I diagnosed that I actually had mono, definitely more than a cold. But at the time I was happy for any diagnosis that would allow me to stop for even a day and rest.

The mono was brought on by a peak of stress caused by the letter I did not want. My girlfriend, who said she would be there for me after boot camp and was looking forward to a new life wherever the Navy sent me, ended our relationship. In her letter she stated that her mother said that I had probably already found another girl. I looked around the all-male division I was training with. Nope. I had not even spoken to a woman in weeks, and the few we had seen were out of reach in other divisions. But her words told me that the girlfriend had been worked over as soon as I left town and had been convinced to give up on us and me. Now I was completely alone. I had been counting on getting my life back after boot camp. I had envisioned all my books and the cats and the comfort of coming home at the end of the day. Now all that was gone. The last ties to my past had been cut.

But likewise, I could not see the future. My belongings were boxed up in Nebraska. I did not know when I would have them again. Without the prospect of marriage, I would not get the housing allowance, so I would not have a place of my own. When I went to the fleet I would be sleeping on the ship instead of my own bed. It was too early in boot camp to get your orders for your next command. In a few weeks I could be sent to anywhere in the world.

Everything was in flux, uncertain, unknown. The only thing to do was focus on the task at hand, moment by moment. Everything else was out of my power. I had no agency in my own life anymore.

After nine weeks, boot camp ended. We graduated, saw our families, and went on to our ships or next schools. The recruits had been turned into service members, warfighters, sailors. We were recognizable on the surface as the people we were before but something had changed. Even those of us who had a soul that ran deep enough to not be truly militarized were now something else. We were sailors and the strange life of the American in the military was completely normal to us now.

The Ship

After another brief school to learn intermediate seamanship I went to Norfolk, Virginia to report to USS Hawes, FFG-53. I walked down the dock to a low, long gray warship, boxy on top but with the narrow and sharp bow of a sub hunter. This wasn't a cumbersome aircraft carrier. The frigates were the last of the tin can Navy.

Immediately I was thrown into another harsh world. I was told to report to the admin office, then treated like an idiot because I did not know where the office was. I had been on the ship less than 30 seconds. The training technique of condescending abuse is common in the military and it takes a thick skin to survive. Much of my later popularity with new shipmates who came after me was due to my refusal to train people through demeaning them.

There was no one in the ship's office. I was given an empty rack to sleep in and left on my own.

The next day I was given a tour of the ship that would be my home and weapon for the next four years. 453 feet long, 53 feet of beam at the widest point and with one massive propeller, the Oliver Hazard Perry class frigate USS Hawes was a 1985-vintage sub hunter of the Cold War. It was designed to be cheap to build and more or less disposable. Intended for escort service and finding Soviet submarines, in the late 80s the class was pressed into patrol and deterrence roles as well. Two ships of the class had been badly damaged in the Persian Gulf during the undeclared "Tanker War" against Iran. One hit a mine and one was hit by an anti-ship missile. Both survived this severe combat damage. For being so cheap, the class had proved to be sturdy and reliable.

After the Cold War ended many of the frigates were used for drug interdiction in the Caribbean and Pacific. They were also good for diplomacy and international exercises with the ability to sail into relatively shallow waters and leave a foreign pier under their own power. After 9/11 and the start of the Iraq War they were used for terrorist hunting in the Arabian Gulf and the north Indian Ocean, and pirate chasing off Somalia.

Originally intended as a jack-of-all-trades the frigates were armed with a 76-mm gun in a turret, a Close-In Weapon System (CIWS, or "sea-wizz") Gatling gun for knocking down missiles, and a missile launching system of its own. By the time I arrived on the dock, the missile system had been removed. Much late-night bridge watch debate revolved around this, arguing whether the ship designation "FFG" (Guided Missile Frigate) should be changed to simply "FF." And with the debut of fears of non-state enemies and asynchronous warfare we were festooned with 40 mm, .50 Cal and 7.62 mm machine guns. These we practiced most of all.

The ship's crew was 230 sailors more or less, depending whether there was an air detail with two helicopters on board or not. The crew was all male, except for two or three women officers. As part of the program to create more gender equality and open more roles to women even a ship like ours, not originally intended to house women, made space for several female officers. It was easier to make space for them in officer country than having a whole berthing dedicated to enlisted women, as the newer ships were able to have, since they were designed for that purpose from the drawing board.

Officer country was small, and not completely inaccessible to enlisted as on bigger ships because you had to pass through it to get from one end of the ship to the other. This, and the generally small crew size, helped keep the atmosphere somewhat egalitarian. For us enlisted our berthing was deep down in the ship under the waterline. The bunks (racks, as they are called) were stacked three high, with not much headroom at the bottom. Small blue curtains could be velcro'd shut for privacy and to block out the light if you had to sleep during the day. Two straps with hooks could be closed in case the seas were heavy so you did not fly out of your rack and hit the deck. The racks could be lifted for storage underneath, and each sailor also had a small upright half-locker for bigger items, especially dress uniforms that you did not want wrinkled. This didn't leave much room for stashing gear for a deployment so sailors that were lucky enough to be in divisions that had a lot of space on the ship, such as the electronics techs and their shop, could keep stuff elsewhere.

I had been assigned to deck division, the group responsible for basic ship maintenance and seamanship duties. We were to moor and unmoor the ship, launch and retrieve small boats, chip a lot of rust and paint, paint, paint. Deck is the largest division on the ship, around 50 sailors. It was hard to stand out and hard to fit in. Usually deck division is populated by those who do not place well on the ASVAB evaluation test and have no intention of going to specialty school. It's the blue-collar division of an enlisted force that is already blue collar.

I was put there as a place-holder before I went to Operations Specialist School. Instead, I got lucky and was plucked from the deck gang to help the quartermasters on the bridge. The QMs (in the Army quartermasters work in supply and logistics; in the Navy the same title is used for navigation) were a small division, only four people not including myself. They needed one more person so they could work a more reasonable watch rotation while out at sea and get some decent sleep.

Having a bachelor's degree in geography, it was a perfect move for me. Immediately I was familiar with the chart table and all its tools, compasses and rulers, protractors for measuring angles and other implements of geometry, geography, and nautical navigation. Endless stacks of charts let me indulge my love of maps. Each one was such an exotic landscape and seascape. I saw places I had not imagined ever getting to see, but now the entire world that touched the sea became a possibility.

There were new tools to learn. Nautical navigation has not changed much over the centuries except for the debut of electronic aids such as LORAN radio navigation and the Global Positioning System. LORAN had already been removed from Navy ships by this time so the main method of determining location was GPS. Along with this modern navigation system, ancient techniques such as taking bearings along lines of direction towards landmarks and navigation markers were still used. When done well this could be more accurate than even GPS, which suffered on occasion from weak signals or the usual vagaries of electronics.

Though it wasn't practiced by all the quartermasters, the tools for celestial navigation, sextants and tables for calculating the angles to the sun, moon, planets and stars were available. The Navy has long gone back and forth on teaching celestial navigation (cel nav for short). Sometimes it is abandoned in the face of overwhelming technology, and sometimes it is taught due to the realization that technology fails or can be degraded by electronic warfare. At the time I was in the service, cel nav was considered advanced training for quartermasters and the officers still learned it as part of their schooling.

I voluntarily worked at cel nav. The feel of the heavy sextant in my hands, the skill of using the arm and mirrors to bring down a celestial object to the horizon to measure the angle, the ceremony of taking a sun line at noon and marking it on the chart, all harked back to the ancient traditions of the sea. A sun line that was dead-on with the GPS fix was satisfying, and gave the awareness-expanding pleasure of being connected to the sun itself.

Underway, my job was to be "Quartermaster of the Watch," responsible for maintaining the ship's position on the chart, indicating the direction of travel, keeping an eye on what was ahead of us, watching and predicting the weather, and giving recommendations to the officer of the deck regarding all the above. I also served as another pair of eyes on the bridge, keeping a lookout and recording all ship's events in the deck log. Usually each shift on watch was five or six hours long. If I was off-watch at night I got to sleep; if I was off-watch during the day I had to clean, maintain equipment, train, or generally be available if my division needed me. That means if I was on watch from midnight to six in the morning I rolled right into a work day and probably went back on watch after dinner. Eight straight hours of sleep at sea was rare.

Training was constant. Force protection (standing guard and shooting at things or people who become unfriendly), damage control, man overboard recovery, helicopter operations, working with other ships as a group, surface combat, air-defense, hunting submarines, being hunted by submarines, chemical, biological and nuclear attack (i.e. wearing a gas mask for hours and being annoyed), search and rescue...the list of subjects to train a crew on was endless. And everything had to be practiced and re-certified every year or so. Even when not deployed, many day and weeks were spent off the coast of Virginia training.

After a year or so I had the thought that I wanted to try to become an officer. I had the education already. The recruiters had told me that they were not recruiting new officers because "there were too many." I learned after a few months that not only was this probably not true, most things you are told about career advancement, whether enlisted or commissioned officer, are not true. The personnel command constantly puts out all sorts of directives and programs and fancy ideas to make the military more like a civilian career. You're told that education is important, or that you can choose a career path or that there are so many cool orders you can take for far-off exotic lands. But out in the fleet none of that amounts to much. Advancement is old school; wait your time, take a test to advance in rate, and hope.

Ambition, if you are enlisted, is viewed in a very Midwest manner: keep your mouth shut, work, and hope the powers above you toss you a bone. Never display ambition. So, starting my campaign to apply for Officer Candidate School (OCS) was difficult. I had to convince a cadre of chief petty officers, the senior enlisted personnel, that instead of putting in my time and climbing the ladder to their position, I instead wanted to become an officer and be in charge of them, perhaps? I believe I stammered out something about greater responsibility than I had now, and I got a begrudging approval from the ship's command master chief.

I had to decide what type of officer I wanted to be. Age was a limit. Being past 30 years old already, becoming a line officer and rising the ranks to command a ship was not an option. I didn't have the educational background or proclivity for engineering. Supply officer corps was, in my mind, glorified retail management. The intelligence group sounded far more interesting to me. My BS in geography was a good fit, and intel called for skills of organization and analysis that I already possessed. So I made the intelligence officer track my goal.

Our captain at that time was more supportive than the chiefs and gladly provided a letter of recommendation. He also arranged for me to interview with a full captain O-6 intelligence officer, which proved to be a fantastic introduction. I was convinced that this was a viable career path for me. The next step was to take the officer candidate test. This was yet another test, similar to the ASVAB taken by potential recruits when they walk into the storefront on that first day at the recruitment center. It was at this point, when arranging the officer test, that the uncertainty and poor definition of personnel regulations struck. The classic military bureaucracy started throwing wrenches in every gear that it could find.

The officer test consisted of several parts, and which parts you took depended on what kind of officer you intended to be. Because intel officers also worked with naval aviation commands there was a chance that I would have to take the aviation portion of the test as well as the core competency section. But no one was sure. Our ship's admins could read the regulation but did not know how to properly interpret it. Our own officers, none of whom were aviation, did not know. Between deployments the Hawes did not have an air detail onboard so we had no aviation officers to ask. Finally, after much emailing of personnel command contacts scraped off Navy websites, I got an answer—I did not have to take the aviation portion.

So, I took the core test and passed, did very well in fact. Good news, and I was able to submit my OCS package. And, of course, after submitting it, I was informed that I also had to take the aviation portion. So back to the test office, another good score, and the extra results sent to personnel command to add to my submission package.

Later that year, while on deployment, I was informed that my submission had been rejected because I had not taken the two parts of the test together. I could, if I wished, take the test again properly and resubmit. However, I had to do so before the cutoff of age 34. I looked at the test schedule for Bahrain, the closest shore command, but we would not be in port on that date. I stepped out on the bridge wing and stared over the slack and sun-seared water of the Gulf of Yemen. There was no way to make it before I aged past the deadline. Because of the confused and poorly defined bureaucracy of the military, I had lost a chance to make a real career in a position of responsibility and prominence. Instead, I was going to be enlisted with no path out. It wasn't the work I wanted to do for the rest of my life.

After being in the military for a while you learn not to trust anything you are told. Near the end of my four years it was time to decide on reenlistment. I had pretty much decided that I would not reenlist, that I wanted out, so I could continue with life. By that time the Navy felt like a giant pause in my arc. However, I told myself and my family that I would at least take a look at the possibilities reenlistment provided. It was a decently paying job, after all, with healthcare and retirement. I had advanced fairly quickly and my Bachelor's degree would get me to at least senior chief (E-8) at a steady pace. Besides getting a civilian job and maybe going back to school I had no defined vision of my post-Navy life. It would not hurt to look into another four years.

The Navy had too many of my rate, so if there was going to be a reenlistment bonus it wasn't going to be much money. The variety of orders were actually interesting. I could finally fulfill those dreams of travel and take orders to Japan or Italy. I could choose to serve on a ship and get more time at sea, but I also could cycle to a shore command and get regular working hours without deployments. That would make it much easier to have a real life again, possibly go back to school while staying in the military. The orders meant getting out of Norfolk and seeing a new city or country, a new horizon.

However. Small ships such as the Hawes are difficult commands to work at, because of the intense pace of sea time and the chronic under-staffing. With such a small crew it only took a few bad or lazy sailors to put a lot of strain on everyone else as they carried the dead weight. Good sailors were valuable and the command was left wanting when they moved on. Because of this, some shipmates who had tried to leave found their new orders mysteriously screwed up somehow. Several sailors had orders to attend SEAL school. After boot camp they were sent to the fleet for a year or so to gain fleet experience then transferred to the school. Because someone with the mindset and work ethic to join the SEALs invariably was an excellent sailor, the command tried to talk them out of their orders, and in one case actively tried to delay the transfer. That shipmate had to get his congressional representative involved to have his orders reinstated so he could go to SEAL school. Another SEAL candidate, after a few months on the Hawes, simply decided the misery of Navy life and bureaucratic incompetence wasn't worth the bother and decided to ride out his time and get out of the Navy altogether when his enlistment was done.

Towards the end of my enlistment it was common for medical screenings to not be scheduled or go missing. These screenings were required to take orders to an overseas command. At that point, if the sailor had already reenlisted, then they would be staying on Hawes for another four years instead of moving on to their dream orders. Instead of taking the risk of picking great overseas orders and having my own medical screening disappear, I decided that it wasn't worth it. I opted to leave the military. I had already learned the lesson: despite all the talk about career paths and advancement and the new, smarter educated Navy, your wishes and dreams meant nothing to the bureaucracy. You either had to be reconciled to a lack of control over your destiny or you had to get out and get your life back.

The life of a ship is the life of a machine, and the sailors are levers and cogs. They must be integrated as much as any other part. But they also are the life of the ship and give it a soul and personality. The cycles of time on the sea and time at the dock slowly merge the lifeless machine and the flesh, blood and minds of the sailors into an indivisible whole.

Shipmates

There are people who join the military due to family tradition or simply because they need a job. Others join because they don't fit in. For some reason or another they can't find a place in American society. I certainly include myself in that clan. The military is an organization of America's best misfits, representing the very country that they can't accept or won't accept them.

The first group of misfits you encounter are your own recruiters. In the Navy recruiting office in Lincoln, Nebraska were several senior sailors enjoying their shore duty close to home. One had just gotten married to a hometown girl, who most likely saw a way out of Nebraska with a steady income and free health care. They had gotten married after only a month because she was pregnant, or so she claimed. It did not take much knowledge of biology to know how unlikely the signs had manifested that quickly. Another recruiter told me that there were too many officers in the Navy so I could not take that route. He also screwed up paperwork that would have paid off my student loans instead of giving me the GI Bill. I imagine none of this was deliberate and vindictive, but it should have warned me immediately that what was promised and what was going to be delivered were two very different things.

Getting to the fleet introduced me to a whole crew of characters. After telling my sad story of being dumped in boot camp to our deck division senior chief he suggested that I start seeing a prostitute, make her a regular thing so I could have the semblance of a relationship without any of the attachment or obligation. I was shocked. I had never known anyone in my life who had paid for sex and besides any moral issues it just struck me as desperately sad to do so to create the semblance of a relationship. I definitely did not take his advice, but it put me on notice that I was in a very different world from the one in which I grew up. Life was rough around the edges for many in the military, both in their old lives before the service and in their new existence as a G.I.

Loneliness was rampant among the younger sailors and there was a variety of ways people handled it. Some got married quickly, either to high school sweethearts or the first willing woman they met after boot camp. These marriages were often unhappy and short. After the novelty wore off, men could not wait to get away to sea. The wives were happy to see them go. Cheating was rampant on both sides. I decided against assuaging my pain by setting up house that way.

Of course, womanizing was popular. Sailors had their reputation and if anonymous sex was desired it took no effort to find someone at the club. Also, not my scene. The few times when I was dragged to a club by shipmates I just stood in a corner and seethed at the overpriced watery drinks and loathed the music too loud to have a normal conversation. Otherwise I avoided clubs like the plague.

If you simply wanted a girlfriend, a real relationship, the odds were against you. Because of that sailor's reputation it was difficult if not impossible to convince someone that you were actually a good, decent human being. You could be talking to someone and see the enthusiasm drain from their eyes once they realized you were a sailor. More likely, since they could tell from the haircut that you were military, no one talked to you at all. This feeling of being on the outside looking in at civilian life gave me my first experiences of exclusion, and what it must be like to be on the receiving end of bigotry.

For those who were below the rank of E-5 and were unmarried, you did not get a housing allowance. This motivated some people to get married just for that extra money. Others, if they did not get some roommates together to rent an apartment, lived on the ship. "Lived" is a relative term. Your car quickly became a pile of civilian clothes and personal items. I kept a storage locker off-base for myriad items such as extra clothes, books, and keepsakes that reminded me of the home I did not have. Nothing makes you feel like you've hit rock bottom in life than changing clothes in a storage unit in the middle of winter.

Since I lived on the ship, the same place I worked all day, as soon as liberty was announced I swapped clothes and made a run for it off base as quickly as possible. Off duty hours were spent driving around the Hampton Roads area. I had a set of chosen hang outs where I could get on the internet for free while being left alone to sit for hours. Panera was often my first stop, for dinner as well as internet. The Borders bookstore was also a haunt, thanks to the uncrowded tables and free internet access. Stella's Coffeehouse in the Ghent district was good, if I could find a place to sit. Stella's and the library at Old Dominion University were places where I could hope to blend with the student population. Off duty, I wanted to pretend to be a civilian for a while.

Some sailors turned their cars into de facto apartments, including sleeping in their cars in the base parking lot to avoid sleeping on the ship. I heard a story about a sailor who kept a TV and xBox in his car and played video games out there, with a cigarette lighter electricity converter. Some simply disappeared, and no one knew where they went when off duty.

That was my first two years in the Navy. Semi-homeless, alone. Nowhere to go. Knowing no one like-minded and considered suspicious by the locals because I was in the military. Those two years were the worst of my life.

In time, I was able to make the rank of E-5 and earn the housing allowance without being married. The first night in my new apartment, my first personal space in two years, I slept on the hardwood floor in a sleeping bag without any sort of cushion underneath me. It was the best sleep of my life. I finally had a space of my own again, and the mental comfort of being able to close a door and lock it and be alone was indescribable. It meant I was on the way to becoming a human again.

Sometimes, the people associated with the military, both within and without, were unsavory. Drugs were always an issue, both sailors using and sailors selling. Several times, someone did not report for duty in the morning because they had been arrested out in town for possession or dealing. It also was a common tactic for sailors to smoke marijuana purposely to get caught on the frequent drug tests. If you popped on the test you would be discharged quickly with an administrative discharge. Those were easy to get upgraded to an honorable discharge with some paperwork and an appeal after a few months out. Or, the discharged sailor simply didn't care and just wanted out of the Navy. Reportedly, at one Captain's Mast (a minor trial onboard under the Uniform Code of Military Justice) our frustrated captain asked the sailor on trial what would possess him to smoke pot. The sailor responded, "I want out and I wonder why it took you so long to bust me."

The life was harsh but there was humor too. The informality of a small ship let us break some rules on occasion and broke down the barriers between enlisted and officers at times so everyone could relax. The bridge watches, with three or so officers and half a dozen enlisted, could be informal when there was no particular task. For a long time on deployment there was a nightly trivia game amongst the bridge watch standers. Even one of our captains got in on the fun. He would sneak onto the bridge in the dark to see how vigilant the watch standers were. It was part of the quartermaster's job to note in the ship's log when the captain entered the bridge, and actually say it out loud: "Captain's on the bridge!" After running across the captain in the dark a few times (one time actually colliding into him, and other times having the flashlight yanked out of my hands, startling me) we made a deal where I would quietly log him as being on the bridge without shouting it out, and he could use the quiet and dark corner of the bridge by the chart table to observe his junior officers at work.

The ship had a system of sound-powered telephones. These ingeniously simple devices date back to the Second World War. Working without electricity, they ensured communication even when the ship's power was knocked out by war or accident and were redundant enough to get a message from bow to stern through multiple channels. They also allowed the lookouts to talk to us on the bridge, and facilitated epic bull sessions when times were slow at sea.

One night across the sound-powered telephone system there was a debate on the relative merits of cats versus dogs as pets. One shipmate, whom I will leave nameless, stated that he hated dogs, which is why he really wanted a husky. Silence on the line. Someone pointed out to him that a husky was a dog. "Oh no man, no, a husky's a cat." The conversation dwindled after that.

You could hate the military, and many of us did. But you could not hate your shipmates who were suffering through it with you. You did the best you could to make time go by for yourself and everyone else. Sometimes the ribbing got vicious. Most of the time the humor helped all of us. Everyone seemed like they were waiting for their enlistment to end, or something better to happen in their lives.

Ports & Travels

They say you can travel the world in the military, and that's true. But don't expect to see the nice parts of it. Or, if you are in the Navy, the parts that are not water.

For many people in the service this is their first time overseas. Often, it may be the only foreign travel they do their entire lives. How they encounter the world, whether they learn and experience or whether they are fearful and closed, may shape their attitude as citizens and humans for the rest of their lives. In some cases, the attitudes they have are what they bring with them and nothing changes. Sometimes, we're told tales before hitting shore meant to scare us, or breed contempt for the local culture. And the rules of port visits often put a barrier between you and the country you are visiting.

When you go ashore you are required to have a "liberty buddy," either one or two other people depending on how dangerous the Navy thinks the country might be. You are not to be separated from these people ever and coming back to the ship at the end of the day without everyone you signed out with meant serious trouble. This also means that whatever the group wants to do has to be negotiated and if you have an interest that no one else wants to pursue then you're pretty much out of luck.

For example, the Hawes visited the port of Chania on the island of Crete five times in one deployment. It became a running joke that the crew should just get apartments in town. The port is a NATO base, so it was cheap to dock there, and the Hawes being a small ship with a captain with little seniority we got the not-so-fun cheap ports while the aircraft carriers got the fun ports. Such is the tin can Navy life. However, I was excited because tours were offered to the Minoan archaeological site of Knossos and the mythical Labyrinth, home of the Minotaur. The tour would only take place if enough people signed up to go, however. I asked, I lobbied, I pleaded, I begged. No one wanted to go.

Five times I went to Crete and never saw Knossos. Never.

I did see a lot of malls. And restaurants. Fortunately, I was able to find the adult crowd on the ship, so I did not see the inside of too many bars and thankfully no whorehouses. But that's the weakness of the Navy shore leave system. You are reliant on the whims of others and if there's something you badly want to see and no one else does you'll never see it. Even in a safe port such as France or Italy the assumption is that you are not responsible enough to be left on your own. As someone who had travelled overseas before the Navy this grated on me considerably. It was difficult being a responsible person in an environment where it is assumed you are not.

But being that responsible person helps when things go wrong. During our port visit to Cannes many shipmates decided to take the train down the coast to Nice. It was a much bigger city with more going on (Cannes is sleepy without the film fest). With a curfew to get back to the ship all of us who were in the city got back to the Nice train station at the same time.

But the trains weren't running. None of us spoke French so we had no idea what was going on. My cell phone worked overseas thanks to AT&T so I called the ship and told them we were stuck and had no idea why. As more shipmates showed up at the station I made a list of who was trapped in Nice. That way at least they would not be in trouble for getting back to the ship late. As the demands from the ship duty officer to know what was going on got more adamant I used gestures to ask a railway worker to talk to the ship and tell them the story in French (a local liaison was on the ship to help handle situations like this). Apparently, a suicide had occurred and stopped all trains for investigation and clean up. Eventually, after many hours (and fending off a shady Brit who was trying to sell us drugs) the trains started and we got home, with everyone accounted for.

The biggest danger overseas is not terrorists but cab drivers. In Crete, a shipmate and I were taking a cab from the base to the old city center on the harbor. The cabbie was yelling into his phone intermittently, making phone calls and taking them. In between calls he told us about how his son's wife had been cheating on him. He kept yelling "women are shit!" His driving became more erratic and we noticed that we were not taking the usual route to the harbor. Finally, in some residential area far off our path he brought the car to a sudden halt and ran into a house. My shipmate and I wondered if we were going to be witness to a domestic disturbance that would be very difficult to explain to the police and our command. Fortunately, after a few minutes the cabbie came out, calmer and apparently without having committed an awkward murder.

Another dangerous cab ride was in Naples. Stuck in an interminable traffic jam with a driver whose ring tone was "I Will Survive" by Gloria Gaynor, we got tired of waiting and asked to be dropped off at the next corner. The cab driver, suddenly afraid of losing a fare, went insane. Side streets, sidewalks, alleys, he used them all to get us to the square we wanted to have lunch at. Coincidentally (or did he phone in the request?) the radio started playing his favorite song. Too appropriate for the madcap drive we were on. One shipmate was visibly shaking after he got out of the car. I had been on my own cell phone talking to my mother the entire time and this is still one of her favorite moments of my Navy time, getting a live narration of the cab ride from hell.

In my four years, the USS Hawes hit port in Savannah, Georgia; Beaumont, Texas; Cannes, France; Maddalena, Sardinia; Valletta, Malta; Naples, Italy; Chania, Greece; Massawa, Eritrea; Muscat, Oman; Dubai, U.A.E.; Manama, Bahrain; and Victoria, Seychelles. Not in that order, and some of them more than once. I left out a couple stops for fuel that had us in port for less than a day or just overnight.

The ports in the U.S. were public relations stops. We gave tours and went around town on liberty to be good sailors and help promote the Navy, military and the flag. As ports, they were safe and good practice for hitting shore for the first time (Savannah was my first port). And because it was U.S. soil we could leave the ship on our own. I once spent a beautiful afternoon sitting on a park bench in one of the classic Savannah town squares, bordered by Antebellum mansions, reading and watching the languid life of the town drift by.

The most difficult and strangest port was Eritrea. Sent to Massawa for a diplomatic visit, we cleaned and painted in horrid 100-degree plus heat in dripping humidity. Fat antibiotic pills served as a prophylactic against malaria exposure. After hours a bus took us into town where the only place to exchange U.S. dollars into local currency was a hotel. After standing for interminable minutes to get Eritrean Nakfa (or as one shipmate called them, "African dollars") we looked around for something to spend them on. In one of the few restaurants in town we ate locally, unique Eritrean/Ethiopian cuisine with injera, the spongy flatbread that accompanies every meal in the region. And that was pretty much it. It was an awkward time in town. The locals seemed nervous, not surprising given the authoritarian nature of the Eritrean government. Some of the local workers who came to the pier to drop off supplies begged us to take them with us. Before pulling away from port the captain ordered a thorough search of the ship for stowaways.

An equally weird port visit was Dubai, at the opposite end of the financial spectrum from Massawa. Dubai was a break from the caldron of the Iraq shore. Going from a combat area to what was essentially Vegas without the gambling resulted in sensory overload. At the main mall there was an indoor ski slope, the sheer ostentatiousness of which stopped me in my tracks. I could not fathom how much energy it was taking to keep that enormous room cold enough for snow. Walking around Tower Records, my senses were bombarded by music and lights and neon. I could not concentrate and even reading the placards organizing the CDs by artist was difficult. It was all overwhelming.

The sheer gaudy wealth was off-putting and fascinating at the same time. A cab driver pointed out the Burj Al-Arab under construction, soon to be the tallest building in the world. Everything was brand new but dusty already from the desert environment. The heat was oppressive and again soaking humid, which is common in the coastal Middle East. The many Asian workers, servants hired from less wealthy countries, seemed to outnumber everyone else.

My liberty buddy group was able to get away from the city for one afternoon and evening. A tour took us bounding over dunes by four-wheel drive out to a desert camp where we would be fed an authentic Middle-Eastern banquet and entertained with music and dancers under the stars. The driver was Pakistani, in Dubai on a work visa and glad for our questions and friendliness. He often did tours for visiting ships and noted that sailors from the smaller ships tended to be friendlier. The difference between small town living versus the insular city folk of the aircraft carriers, perhaps. The banquet camp was predictably touristy but the food was superb and being able to walk away from the campfire a few steps and stand on Arabian sand, staring up at the stars, grounded me to a place far from home. I could feel the depth of ancient sand underneath my feet.

The port I loved the most was Muscat, Oman. Oman is peaceful, quietly prosperous, and does not participate much in the affairs of others. The gaudiness of Dubai is nowhere to be seen. The pushy mercantilism of Bahrain can't be found here either, and it's possible to casually stroll through the old souk without salesmen in your face.

We did, of course, go to the mall. The country was considered safe enough that some shipmates had the option of getting hotel rooms for a night or two, though I did not take that option (230 roommates was enough; I didn't want another one for one night). A small group of us had an exquisite meal at Trader Vic's, splurging some of the accumulated cash that builds up over months at sea. When someone left their wallet in a cab, the driver turned around and came back to the pier to return it. Oman is that kind of place.

That's what travel in the Middle East teaches you. I wish that our government could buy one round-trip ticket to any Middle Eastern country for every American. Unlike the endless fear that we are presented with in our media, they could see for themselves that there are many safe and peaceful places and friendly people. There are dangerous people and yes, they are Muslim. The dangerous people are fewer than you think outside of the war zones. Most Muslims, like most folks anywhere, just want to get on with their lives without much bother. That human experience is universal.

The best lesson came from people watching in a mall in Dubai. Once I watched a Muslim woman, high-end fashion jeans jutting out of her ankle-length abaya, stride with purpose. This was a woman on an unstoppable shopping mission. Behind her, a servant pushed an empty stroller. Behind the servant, dressed in the traditional thawb and keffiyeh, walked the husband, carrying the baby.

Patriarchal society, indeed. It was a reminder that while we all have our cultures that give us a base of beliefs and behaviors, each human is also an individual who will have a unique path through life with their own experiences. These make each of us our own person. Culture is only the start. If you want to know what anyone is about, don't assume from their culture. Just ask, one human to another.

The Wilderness

The Sea.

The sea.

Armies fight on land, increasingly in cities where the things they smash are familiar—streets, buildings, houses, and innocent people. Outside the city they fight in fields and mountains, farms and deserts. Everyone knows what those are. Walking on the ground is the same anywhere, even if the surface of the landscape and the culture seems strange. People know human lands and human things, no matter where they go.

But navies fight on the sea, the largest wilderness on Earth. Here, no human goes except temporarily. We are alien on the ocean and do not belong. Only through will and need do we venture into that realm and can only live there through great effort and frequent supply. We do not belong there and can never stay. The sea swallows our warfare into its depths. It cannot be conquered or held like land. And in a capricious mood it can be more dangerous than any human opponent.

But to those who can watch the sea with eyes unfocused from human concerns, the sea will show them a world primordial and pure. If you spend enough time at sea and are willing to let go of the human voice that chatters away in your self-awareness, you can start to belong to the sea as well as to the land.

I have seen the ocean in so many moods. Off the coast of Virginia, it is deep blue with white foam flakes at the top of peaky waves on a blustery spring day. When still and overcast the silver clouds reflect deeply on a glass surface that you ache to disturb with the ship's bow. In the shallows approaching Bahrain the dusty light blue surface hides a hazard of sandbanks, and you must steer precisely to avoid the trap the barely-ocean the Gulf has made. There are towering tropical clouds at the equator, pink with the sun's end-of-day light as it sinks. The Mediterranean is beautifully blue and feels larger than it should. A winter sea challenges the ship's presence on the wilderness, most of all at night when you cannot even see the waves that crash into you. The wind wraps itself around the mast and pushes the ship over, so the decks never straighten. I would wrap myself deeper into my coat and be glad the wind made it too loud to talk. I felt safe from the sea even though in my heart I knew that I was not. And I dared not think about the depths under my feet.

Despite the dynamic beauty of the ocean, not every day on the sea is different. In certain seasons there is a stultifying sameness for days or weeks or months. In the North Atlantic springtime with a gentle sun and breeze, the uniformity is pleasant. Watch-standing is comfortable, almost somnolent. A week goes by easily and pleasantly. It's a pleasure to be out Monday and back in time for the weekend. Conversation flows lightly and without barriers of rank and rate. All are happy to be on a calm water and duties are easy.

In contrast, the monotony of the monsoon off Somalia, with an endless march of uniform rolling waves, 20 feet high with a trough the same width in between, evenly spaced for thousands of miles, wears out sailors and ships. No point on the compass is smooth. The dust-hazed sun softens shadows so the entire day seems one long hour. You forget how long you've been there, and forget that someday you'll leave.

Other times the sea is wild. The ocean is always moving two directions at once. This is called "set and drift," and monitoring this and taking it into account in the ship's movement is vital for a quartermaster. The water can be moving one direction, whether from currents or distant storms. The air above the water can be moving another direction, directly against the current or at an angle. This creates the chop and waves that can make a voyage uncomfortable or pitch your ship every which way in chaos. Regardless, if it's not measured and watched the ship can end up in a very different place than planned. The movement of a ship across water is at the mercy of the weather, and technology and human will shall be frustrated often.

The strangest seas I have ever seen were off the coast of Virginia and North Carolina one winter. The air was just above freezing, as was normal for winter, but we were at the edge of the Gulf Stream sailing in 70-degree water. The cold air started to draw fog from the ocean surface, first wispy and a few feet above the water, then thickening to obscure the sea and rise to the same height as the ship's railing. We were sailing on a cloud.

Off our port bow back towards land waterspouts started to form, dozens of them. Some small ones were close by but the large ones that could have damaged the ship stayed thankfully far away. Our captain told us to keep an eye out for Sirens, the mythical creatures that lured sailors to their doom on jagged rocks. Master Chief, who had always served on aircraft carriers, marveled like a kid at the natural spectacle of being right in the middle of the cloud and the waterspouts and the rest of the ocean's theater. The wonder of the sea resets and equalizes military discipline until every sailor of any rank is simply an overawed human on a very large ocean.

The powerhouse of the ocean is the sun. It creates the winds and hence the waves. On a spring day the sun feels nice, as a herald of the end of winter. A warm sun and a cold breeze combine perfectly and watch standing is a happy time, exposed to the natural world in the joy of spring. During the summer or in the hot latitudes there is no shelter from its burning face except that which you bring with you. A winter sun can be kind, but at times clouds of winter are welcomed so that your eyes are comfortable, even if the meeting between sky and water is not clear. The mood of the sun for the day can set the pace of work, how far the lookouts see, and the mood of the crew. A kind sun is joyful. A sun like a hammer oppresses everyone.

In Middle East waters the sun is evil. Without shelter, the sun on the sea is overwhelming, desiccating, and demanding. The heat is indescribable and there is no wind to allay it. Every step outside the shade of the pilot house exposes you to the pressing weight of light and heat. No matter how beautiful the sea is in those latitudes the sun reminds you that it is a desert and without the artificial womb of your ship it will kill you quickly. The exposure of the tropics is no more survivable than that of the arctic. Falling into the water is no comfort and would kill you just as quickly. I dreaded day watches and looked forward to the nights when the sun would not burn me, and I could see the stars.

The darkest skies I have seen were while on the ocean. On my second deployment we got south of the equator and saw the Southern Cross and other artifacts of the strange southern night. Twice we experienced lunar eclipses, unexpected until they started and the lookouts reported the moon disappearing. With skepticism I stepped onto the bridge wing to find myself also witnessing the moon being eaten. I had to get on to the Naval Observatory website through very slow satellite internet to run our latitude and longitude through the online astronomical calculators to see what was going on, and to check the bulletins. Naturally, the Observatory knew the eclipses were going to happen but oddly they never sent out notices to the ships in the fleet.

The lookouts made good astronomy students. I had them point the "Big Eyes" mounted binoculars up to look at the mountains and craters of the Moon, or the Andromeda Galaxy. Even the night vision scope made for an interesting astronomical device, enhancing dim stars and wispy nebulae in glowing green electronic renditions. For some of these kids, who grew up in cities with constant light pollution, this was the first time they had ever really looked up at the night sky. Listening to their excitement brought me joy at their fascination, even if they should have been looking out instead of up. I enjoyed showing them something unofficial but poignant and distracting them from military duties.

Everyone wants to see a whale. Or dolphins. Dolphins were common, either swimming near the ship in large groups hunting fish or, if the speed was on, playing in the ship's bow wave. They always drew us to the rails to watch. Whales were rare, and a surfacing with a large blow drew an exclamation from anyone who was lucky enough to spot it. Their exhalations and inhalations were quick and by the time you ran to the rail to look they were gone. Once they went down they stayed down, longer than the attention spans of the humans waiting for them to resurface. Our interest in the whales was also professional. Hitting a whale could result in serious damage to the ship as well as to the whale, so avoiding that was a duty. The chart table had a card that was supposed to allow us to identify the whale species by the shape of its spout, though the accuracy was extremely questionable. As the whales dove and resurfaced hundreds of yards away they served as reminders of the depths below our feet, and the ship felt that much smaller for a moment.

The first time seeing flying fish, previously a mythical creature to me, was a moment of wonder. It took a few sightings to realize that the mysterious ripples across a calm Atlantic surface were something alive as they dip and dive and scatter. They don't seem real; then they become as common as robins. Another piscine encounter was with the huge sunfish. Rare according to scientists, we saw a fair amount of them off the coast of Virginia, slowly swimming with their tall fins piercing the water and making for false reports of sharks.

The animals that intrigued me the most were the small ones far from any shore. Often in warmer parts of the world we would pass mats of yellow-green seaweed that bobbed and spun as the ship pushed the water aside. Underneath the mats small fish could be seen hiding in the shade and white crabs crawled on top. I wondered about their lives. So far from land, were they born on the seaweed? Did they spend their entire lifecycle never seeing the land, not even knowing what firm ground was? What a small world it must be for them.

My one disappointment in my ocean travels was the lack of birds. On occasion, near land, one would visit us, a dull sparrow or the like hopping about the deck. But we never saw the great sea birds, no albatrosses or terns or petrels. Those dwell mostly in the high latitudes. Few birds seem to have colonized the searing desert waters of the Middle East.

Months go on. Life at sea becomes routine, the ship and the circle of horizon is the entire world. In time, the ship and its sailors become just another ocean creature. We live out here like they do, and our affinity is for the landless life, not the half-forgotten world of the city and teeming noise of humanity thrashing to fulfill its self-appointed meanings. The simplicity of the sea and sky are a world more fundamental and real.

One day off Somalia I watched a tiger shark float along with our ship. The refractions of light through the waves banded the shark in counterpoint to its own stripes, dazzling the silhouette. We both were patrolling the shallow water, her for fish and turtles and us for terrorists.

We mutually had our focus on our prey, the focus that only a predator could bring to the task. Such is the conversion of humans into predators by the expectation of violence.

Combat

In the Navy, combat is rare. With a fleet that is dominant far beyond any other country's capacity there has not been a ship-to-ship conflict for the U.S. Navy since the Tanker War with Iran in the 1980s. In the blue water Navy (as opposed to the SEALs or SeaBees or Hospital Corpsmen who are assigned to combat zones on land) you are far more likely to be killed by falling overboard in heavy seas than enemy action.

So, when I speak of combat I am talking about the near-combat situations that a small ship such as the USS Hawes found itself in: pirate patrol off Somalia, guarding the oil terminals off Iraq, boarding and searching civilian vessels, or shadowing other navies as they move through the same waters. These near-combat situations call for the same preparedness and mindset as a hot action, with the assumption that hostilities can break out any moment. You hope that no one on the other side makes that decision. Sometimes, the people on your side wish to make that decision themselves.

One reason to send a small ship to the Middle East is to perform VBSS—"Visit, Board, Search and Seizure." A small group of volunteers from our crew received extra training in small arms, were issued body armor and other combat gear, and were tasked with stopping small civilian vessels and boarding them. The idea was to look for contraband, especially armaments being smuggled to terrorists, or so the idea went. Sometimes the boarding team went over to a ship just for public relations reasons, to hand out food and water and flyers touting the advantages of U.S. Navy protection on the high seas. The only contraband our team found was some cigarettes and alcohol, hardly our concern, so we let the boat go. I never heard of any VBSS team anywhere in the Navy actually finding anything.

The VBSS capabilities could be used for humanitarian purposes as well. One day while patrolling off the coast of Yemen, the Hawes sailed at a few lazy knots past a group of fishermen. The local boat, the dhow, is wooden-hulled with a high prow and wide stern. The modern dhows all have engines and gave up their traditional sails long ago but the basic shape remains the same. They are ubiquitous in the region.

It was another hot and windless day and the crew was bored. The watchstanders weren't paying attention. One of the officers had made up a gameshow-like trivia contest with the enlisted to make the time go by. The bridge-to-bridge radio was turned low, against the rules, but the constant chatter of ships and boats was annoying to listen to full blast. The radio channel is supposed to be used for conveying navigation information and emergencies only but in most of the world it's used for bullshitting, blasting music at each other and shouting racist jibes at other ships. Picking out something significant from all the nonsense took a lot of concentration.

At my station by the chart table on the starboard side of the bridge I was nearest to the radio and heard a call for help. Very quietly someone was calling to the U.S. Navy vessel, which had to be us as we were the only one in the area. I got the attention of the officer of the deck. The fishing boat that was hailing us had run out of fuel and food and was almost out of water. Sadly, none of the other fishing boats around them would help. Our boarding team went over with a translator and our Corpsmen to provide assistance. We gave them food and water, gassed them up, and pointed them the direction home. If we had not done so, if I had not heard the faint call on the radio, it's likely they would have died out there.

Some humanitarian help came too late. For a while,

Somali refugees had been showing up on the shores of Yemen but no one knew how they were getting there. This was in 2007, before the Yemeni civil war, so Yemen was a safer place than Somalia relatively speaking. The USS Hawes was sent to the Gulf of Aden to figure out how they were getting across the water. Were they taking small boats on their own, or was it more organized?

We found them, as they were returning from Yemen. Two small plastic-hulled boats with bright tarps covering the tops, similar to life boats. The human traffickers had taken the life savings of these Somalis to smuggle them to Yemen. The previous night they had reached the Yemen shore, only to be met by the military. They opened fire. Some Somalis had already made it to shore but the smugglers turned their boats around and fled, leaving them to their fate. When we encountered them in the morning they were on their way back to Somalia, still full of refugees.

The VBSS team geared up and went over. The smugglers were terrified that they were going to be arrested. The refugees, who had spent all their money for nothing, begged us to take them. Some jumped in the water, either to swim to the ship or threatening to kill themselves, I do not know. There were horrendous gunshot wounds from the Yemeni fire and the Corpsmen went over to patch up the wounded. The boats smelled, and the bilges swished with blood and excrement and garbage.

Eventually the VBSS team came back. Some were crying and were ridiculed for their humanity by others who did not go over there themselves. Emasculated by those who weren't brave enough to face the situation themselves. Seeing that level of human suffering and knowing that we could do so little to help them was wrenching. There was nothing shameful in weeping for the injured, the frightened, the desperate, the poor. It was the most human thing the team could do, after helping the refugees with their immediate physical needs.

We could not take the refugees with us. We had been asked by the United Nations to investigate the migration but had not been given a mandate to rescue them from the sea. Giving aid was a basic requirement by the law of the sea and basic human kindness. And being a frigate, and there being so many refugees, we had no room for them. After providing help and collecting intelligence, the USS Hawes sailed away. We were just one very small ship.

Somali waters are also the place to encounter pirates. One Sunday afternoon, as the crew enjoyed a Steel Beach Picnic on the flight deck, the MV Rosen started to head through an area of known pirate activity off the Horn of Africa. The military command in charge of the area asked the small cargo ship if they wanted an escort. They declined. Hours later the ship was seized by pirates.

Being the nearest vessel and the ship that would have escorted them had they taken our offer, the USS Hawes had the job of shadowing the hijacked ship down the Somali coast to the pirate headquarters at Hobyo. This was before Western naval ships were allowed in Somali territorial waters to chase pirates, and before SEAL teams flew out to perform rescue operations. Only deterrence was allowed. With the Rosen already seized there was nothing we could do except watch and report.

Naturally we had manned our guns as soon as we hove into range of the Rosen in case the situation became more belligerent. One of our helicopters was always in the air, watching the Rosen through a zoom lens on the infrared camera so we could see what was happening day or night. As we approached Hobyo, the pirates came on the radio demanding that our helicopter stay away or they would start shooting prisoners. After watching the tiny abstraction of the Rosen on the horizon for a day it was chilling to hear an enemy's voice over the radio. The helicopter was ordered to land. The pilot asked if they could do "bounces," a series of landings to keep their practice up and hit the numbers they needed to keep flight certified. At this lack of sensitivity for the situation the captain utterly blew up, made his order adamant, and called the air detachment officer to the bridge to shout at him as well. The helicopter landed swiftly and no prisoners were injured or killed. The Rosen anchored off Hobyo. After another day, with nothing more to do, we were given permission to sail away and leave the Rosen and her crew to their fate.

While we were shadowing the Rosen to the pirate lair, the incident made international news. Immediately after that we went into combat mode and all outgoing email to friends and family stopped. This was both to preserve satellite bandwidth for vital communications to and from fleet command, and to make sure that nothing classified or sensitive was communicated to the outside world by the crew. Despite this, my parents had a pretty good idea where the USS Hawes was at any time. They started sending me articles from the BBC about the Rosen. The articles only said "US Navy frigate" but it wasn't difficult to figure out which frigate it was. The BBC seemed to know more about the situation than we did, even with reports from 5th Fleet intelligence in Bahrain being sent to us.

As we were following the Rosen down the coast the captain mused out loud that we had no idea where the pirates were taking the Rosen. I mentioned Hobyo, because it was in the BBC article. The captain turned around and gave me a glace. I said my parents had been sending me articles, which made the glace turn into a full stink eye. I stammered something to the effect that my family could guess where we were and that I wasn't sending them anything, then quickly turned back to my chart table.

Similar to these near-combat situations, if due only to

the intensity of effort, was search and rescue. These happened both in home waters and overseas. One night we circled a fishing boat off Florida as they waited for the Coast Guard to come out and tow them home. USS Hawes performed many little assists of that nature. International law requires any vessel to come to the aid of any other vessel without hesitation, and it is a task the Navy takes seriously.

The most eerie search and rescue occurred off the coast of Oman. Our port visit in Dubai was cut slightly short by a typhoon that was plowing through the north Indian Ocean. Ships had been lost and we had to sortie out to help find them. Late at night, with much of the crew not exactly sober since they had been summoned back to the ship from liberty, we unmoored and headed out into the darkness.

We went looking for one ship in particular that had lost contact. After some searching we found it, listing to one side but otherwise intact. Attempts to hail them failed and the boarding team was sent over.

The boarding team described it later as a haunted house. The ship was fine but the engines had stopped. There was no one on board. One of the life boats was missing and it seemed like the crew had abandoned a perfectly good ship, albeit with non-functional engines, to take their chances in the storm. No one ever found them. They had vanished. We radioed in the ship's location and left it to be towed to port by salvagers.

Being in a "hot" fight in the blue water Navy is rare, but shots are fired almost daily in one region of the sea. In shallow water off the coast of Iraq are two oil terminals, KAOT and ABOT. This is where the giant oil tankers dock and take on Iraq's oil, providing an important source of hard currency revenue for the country. This also makes the terminals high value targets for terrorism.

Complicating the situation is the Iranian Revolutionary Guard, who also operate in the area on small motor skiffs. They like to shake down the local fishermen for "tolls" and try and goad reactions from the ships guarding the oil terminals. They frequently came across the border at full speed, zipping in and out of the protective zone and triggering alerts and warning shots. Most likely it was to test and observe our responses. Sometimes it was single boats but on at least one occasion they came over in waves, practicing their own drills in case of the order to perform a real attack. This sort of asymmetrical warfare, where a small boat could be used to attack and damage a much larger, complicated and expensive warship, constantly worried the Navy's military planners ever since the USS Cole had been hit and nearly sunk. Not too long before the Hawes reported to the area, a dhow packed with explosives and sailing towards the terminals had been intercepted by a small Coast Guard boat. The dhow was detonated prematurely and several Coasties had been killed. Even as recently as a few weeks before we showed up a British small boat crew had been seized by Iran and temporarily held prisoner. These incidents, carefully described to us in briefings on our way up the Gulf, were used to sharpen our sense of danger and duty.

Along with U.S. ships, British and Australian ships also guarded the platform. Ships spent a month or two at the platforms then rotated out, the intense situation straining crews and equipment quickly. When the Hawes was assigned to the terminals, the area command was Australian. Their attitude was somewhat more relaxed than our captain's. The Aussies worried about relations with the local fishermen, while our captain was zealous in his duty to protect the terminals at any costs, almost paranoid. His aggressiveness eventually caused problems for us.

We spent some time guarding a pie-shaped sector at each platform, rotated seemingly at random. Onboard, the watch rotation became more intense and navigating in shallow waters near the border of an antagonistic country demanded relentless situational awareness and extreme accuracy at the chart table, lest the Hawes run aground or stray into Iranian waters. The railing-mounted machine guns were loaded and ready to go at a moment's notice. Everyone on watch knew their place when battle stations were called to deal with an incident, either with the Iranians or a civilian boat violating the protection zone. My part, along with keeping the chart table and the deck log and providing navigation information to the officer of the deck, was to work the spotlight next to the bridge wing gunner and keep it on the offending dhow.

During the day not much happened. It was hot and uncomfortable and except for the more intense watch standing it was much the same as being in a patrol box anywhere else in the region. We watched the Revolutionary Guard watch us and listened to sporadic radio traffic.

Nights were different. When there was no moon we had to rely on radar or the infrared video camera on the helicopter to see what was happening around us. The local fishing boats rarely had lights, and when they did it was not in any standard configuration, so it was difficult to identify them. Most of our intercepts happened at night when the dhows, with no lights and no modern navigation equipment, inadvertently cut across the protection zone while trying to get home. We would rush up, horn and loudspeaker blaring, pinning them with a spotlight and firing warning shots. Sometimes we fired "flash-bangs," essentially large firecrackers launched from a shotgun. Some of our more cruel watch standers made a game of trying to set the dhow's canvas awnings on fire with the flash-bangs. Other times it took rounds from the M-60 machine gun or a .50-caliber to get the boat to turn around. These encounters were short, intense, confusing and, for the civilians, completely terrifying. They often simply did not know where they were and shouting threats over a loud speaker while simultaneously shooting at them made their confusion worse.

The locals complained to the area command and we were ordered to tone down our aggression. While there was always the real possibility of a threat to ourselves or the oil terminals our captain was treating every lost fishing boat as a potential attack. The stress on the locals was poisoning relations. To spend a night fishing, worried about a shakedown by the Iranians, just to be attacked by the Americans on the way home, meant no one was on their side. They were caught in the middle of two powers.

In the post-invasion guerilla war the land forces in Iraq were facing, it was very difficult to distinguish friend from foe. Choices of survival had to be made instantly, which led to fear, frustration and savage acts and mistakes. But to me it seemed that with the slower pace of the dhows it was possible to assess the situation better and determine who was a potential danger and who was a lost fisherman. Iranian Revolutionary Guards were obviously always a potential danger and moved at us swiftly, requiring a swift response. A lost fishing boat that was doing its best to get out of our way and turn around after we pulled up to them probably called for an escort and a calm point in the right direction instead being assaulted in a terrifying spectacle of sound and fire.

This war-like stance did not extend to the whole ship. Aft of the mess deck the ship was occupied by supply and administrative divisions. For these sailors daily life never changed much. They did not stand watches but instead worked regular eight-hour days with evenings off and enjoyed an undreamed-of luxury for the rest of us: a full night's sleep, every night. This dichotomy against the "pointy" end of the ship with the Combat Information Center and bridge with their outward-facing, fighting divisions made for some strange encounters. You could come off watch on the bridge, covered in dust and smelling of gunpowder, to see people calmly playing cards on the mess deck and complaining of all the rocking going on as we chased another intruder and potential threat.

These aft-end divisions were big on the spit and polish, probably because they had the time to spit and polish. One night, taking a break from the bridge after an interdiction, I went to the vending machine on the mess deck. One inviolate rule of the mess deck is that you do not cover your head. Whatever hat you are wearing (or cover to use Navy parlance) must be removed. I just wanted to get a quick bite to eat and it was late, so I left my hat on. I figured no one would be around. We had just gone through an intense few minutes of chasing a dhow and the flash of the flares was still in my eyes.

I heard someone say something behind me as I was working the vending machine. A supply division chief petty officer was standing there. He said something about me wearing my cover on the mess decks and the general condition of my unpolished, dust-covered coveralls. Instead of responding as I was supposed to, with some promise to clean myself up, I just stared at him. I literally could not understand what he was talking about. I heard the words clearly but they made no sense, not when I still had the sound of machine guns echoing in my mind. He said a few more things then, realizing that I was simply staring at him with no intention of submission, he turned around and walked away.

One of the long watches from night into day, travelling temporally from the strange hours after midnight into the familiar morning, found us sailing on Mars. Even before the sky started to lighten we knew something was odd. It was difficult to breathe. Visibility had never been great in the area but this night it seemed particularly bad. Dust was accumulating on the chart table and had to be swept off.

By full light, the magnitude of the dust storm was awe-inspiring. Red dust cast everything in a bloody light. An extra look-out was posted on the bow to help see forward, since the world disappeared within a few feet in any direction. Radar seemed to work still but it was suspect. The ship was covered in dust, the sailors were covered in dust, and I alternated between breathing in the horrid material or feeling like I was drowning behind a paper painting mask. This was when the Iranians decided to challenge us.

In their small skiffs with brash engines we could hear them but not see them until they were far too close. It was apparent that they were taking advantage of the dust storm to scout the area, test us, and practice their plans to attack the oil terminals. They were bold enough that the usual warning shots from the machine guns did not phase them. To get them to finally turn, a few shots from a pedestal-mounted 40 mm gun—something in between a machine gun and a large caliber naval gun—was the only weapon impressive enough (and loud enough) to get them to back off.

The USS Hawes spent two months total, over two different stints, at the oil terminals. I stood watch after watch, observing the action around me and doing my part to keep the ship in safe waters. I was content with navigation and entering events in the deck log, and to let the gung-ho younger sailors man the guns and shoot the flares and enjoy the adrenaline. It did nothing for me. One night, in the chaos of yet another encounter with a lost dhow, it was my turn.

The Hawes moved to block a dhow moving into the protection zone. I had stepped out to the starboard bridge wing to man the searchlight. The dhow was less than 100 feet away at that point. The loud speaker was already blaring, and flash-bangs were being fired rapidly. Somehow, instead of making it to the searchlight, I got tapped to man the M-60 machine gun. Without hesitation I stepped up to the gun and started to look down the sight, even though my stomach felt sour. The goal was to be ready for warning shots, so I trained the gun to point in front of the tall prow of the dhow. Warning shots were never directed at the vessel itself but were meant to fall harmlessly into the nearby water. But, with our maneuvers and theirs both ships were pitching wildly, and it was impossible to keep the barrel pointed at the water. The gun kept slewing over the other ship, its deck, prow, pilot house. On the bow stood an old man, dressed all in white, glowing Goya-like in the piercing beam of the searchlight. He waved his arms at us, perhaps to indicate that they were harmless or prevent a collision by will alone. As the ships pitched, my gun kept tracking over him and I fought to keep him out of my sights. If I was given the order to fire there was an excellent chance I would accidentally spray the dhow and hit the old man.

The captain had come onto the bridge at some point and stood next to me. He put his hand on my left shoulder and told me to fire. I paused, then drew a deep breath. I was about to fire when the captain stopped me, as he remembered that we had not been given permission yet to fire warning shots. I breathed hard. A few minutes later I was relieved off the gun by a gunner's mate and gladly retreated to the bridge to get caught up on my chart and deck log.

There are soldiers with much worse stories of war, the death of comrades and the carnage of civilians caught in the crossfire. I don't want my little few moments of near-combat to detract from the true suffering of others with darker stories. But for myself, that is as close as I would like to get to war. If I had manned the gun to return fire at an actual enemy, that would have been one thing. I would have been defending the ship, my shipmates and myself. But looking down the barrel at an innocent man, lost and terrified, and knowing that one wrong pitch of the ship would have meant me accidentally cutting him down, was enough. There was no thrill or sense of power. I only wanted to be anywhere else at that moment. I always knew that the military life was an awkward fit. But in that moment, I knew for sure that I wanted nothing more to do with it.

ANTI-WAR

Entering the Stream

It was the holiday season, 2005. After two long years of living on the ship I had signed a lease for a small apartment of my own, in the Ghent area of Norfolk. This little art neighborhood (what today we would call "hipster") housed many college students from Old Dominion University, wealthier residents of the city, and military personnel trying to blend into normal civilian life. Ghent was a hangout for me when off duty and so I jumped at my chance to move into a place of my own and rebuild a life. The wait between the signing of the lease and picking up my keys in February 2006 was excruciating. It did not matter. I finally had a home again.

My spirits were high and I felt like giving to the world again, instead of defending myself from it. I wanted to buy presents for everyone. And not just typical stuff but something unique, presents that took effort. The First Lutheran Church on Colley Avenue was holding a Christmas market, the Fair Trade Festival, and I went, hoping to pick up a few things for the family. The market featured crafts from refugees and the economically disadvantaged all over the world. I loved this sort of stuff, it let me help people and inspired some mental travel as well.

Along with the tables for merchandise there were also a few organizations handing out pamphlets, talking to folks and publicizing their causes. One table, manned solo, was for Veterans for Peace. Behind it stood a middle-aged man about my height, round glasses and a keen bright look in his eyes. I felt myself being sized up immediately and that he would not take a reluctance for eye contact as a refusal.

He asked me if I were military. I briefly tried to pretend I was not.

Nope, he laughed. It's the haircut. Always gives it away.

He asked me what I thought about the war. Oddly, perhaps because of my good mood, the holiday season, or his open-faced earnestness, I answered honestly. I was opposed to the war but had not thought much about it, even though I had joined in the middle of it.

He then invited me to meet with him and some other local anti-war activists. It turned out that he was hosting a lecture being put on by Amnesty International in a few days, one I had already planned on attending. He wondered if I would be willing to stand up and say a few things.

And that's how I met Tom Palumbo.

*

It was an odd thing to do, in retrospect. I disagreed with the Iraq War. I knew the reasons given to justify the war were lies. I thought it was a horrid idea and the misery it was causing in Iraq was inexcusable. I had even disagreed with the war in Afghanistan. Yes, the Taliban who attacked us were there, so invading made sense. But the neo-conservatives had bungled it badly. They were uninterested in the nation-building that would prevent the Taliban from having any more political influence. The foreign policy issues that had led to 9/11, the United States' support of various hardline regimes and various other forms of meddling to suppress democracy movements in the name of anti-Communism, were not being changed. Nothing was done in support of the common people on the street. Unsurprisingly, when you kicked a people for long enough they kicked back. The claims of innocence in American foreign politics were laughable, if you knew the real history.

I disagreed but took no action to oppose. That is to say, I wasn't politically active outside of voting every four years. Maybe I would vote in a midterm election but didn't think much about it before then or after. I had written to senators and representatives at the Federal level before, about environmental issues mostly. For the greatest events of the mid-2010s in American history I had remained silent, though. In fact, I had volunteered to join the military with the risk that I would become personally embroiled in a military mess that made me angry and disappointed in my country. Why?

Like many decisions in my life it takes a while for the real reasons to come to the surface. There have always been subconscious currents that shape the routes I take. On the surface there are rational reasons and I think things through. But it often takes hindsight years later to see those other currents.

At the time, my rationalization was that I was entering the Navy and therefore I would be safe. There were a few Navy personnel in land combat roles: Seabee construction battalions, SEALs, and Corpsmen stationed with the Marines. But by choosing a sea rate I figured I would have little chance of being in-country facing combat. I would not have to be part of the war I disagreed with.

The other reason is a feature of Midwestern culture. In the Midwest you do not rock the boat. You conform, you do not go too far out of the mainstream, you laugh at the standard jokes, you root for the expected sports teams. In your career you do not show ambition. You hunker down and do your job and wait for those above you to throw you a bone. Authority knows better than you and you don't ask questions. Midwesterners do have an innate sense of fairness and respect for others so, when pushed into the last corner, they will stand up. But it takes a lot to get them there. On a day-to-day basis, their preference is to keep their heads down and get through life.

But. Though being from the suburbs of Chicago and steeped in the passive-aggressive Midwestern ways, I was raised a bit different. My mother marched for the Equal Rights Amendment (which is still out there waiting to be ratified). When I was young, my sister and I attended a rally with Mom for Adlai Stevenson III's run for governor in 1982, and we saw Carol Moseley Braun speak at Harper College during her Senate campaign in 1992. From these political involvements, my sister and I learned how to march, how to organize, and how to stand up. Along with serving as an elected (non-partisan) commissioner on the Palatine Park District board, my sister also worked on the Kucinich campaign and was involved in the League of Women Voters and Code Pink during the wars. My father is generally not an overtly political person, but he is most certainly an original thinker. From him my sister and I learned how to listen and read carefully and think critically about what you heard or read. Forming your own opinion and not accepting the common wisdom has always been his way and I inherited it thoroughly. Being an iconoclast was a badge of honor. With family like this, is it any wonder that I would join the antiwar movement while in the military? I could force myself into conformity for only so long.

I was determined to rock the boat, or in the case of a sailor, the ship.

*

One of Palumbo's projects was an underground newspaper called The Southern (((i))). The first issue came out in January of 2006. Published monthly it was mostly op-ed pieces, a forum for anti-war editorials inspired by the Vietnam War-era anti-war papers. The paper was also part of a wider organization, the Hampton Roads Independent Media Coalition, working to bring news reporting back locally through grassroots efforts. A woman who worked on the paper, Alma Kesling, also ran a short-range local radio station, WRFN, that covered her neighborhood, for example. Along with opinion pieces aimed at the Iraq and Afghanistan wars the paper carried pieces about larger issues of world peace (the attempted coup in Venezuela was mentioned often) and reviews of local events that addressed violence, world peace, social justice and similar issues.

Palumbo and the other staff (all volunteer; there was a financial backer of some sort who paid for the printing of the paper) were excited to have an active duty military member on the paper. I originally performed simple layout and editing duties. My name was on the masthead and it was a good feeling to be involved in something creative and civilian, and the group was a needed social outlet after the isolation of my first two years in the military. Being around independently-minded folk who were the opposite of the military life I was enmeshed in freed me to start acting like myself again. I could discuss politics, books, culture, openly and freely. I felt like a gag had been ripped from my face. Even my own inner monologue became less furtive.

Eventually, I started writing as well. There was much I wanted to say about the wars but being active duty speaking out directly was dicey. I could do so under certain circumstances and within strict rules, such as not in uniform and not claiming any official capacity. Still, the idea made me nervous. But surrounded by the passion of the anti-war movement I decided to take a step.

For the February 2006 issue I wrote "An Open Letter to the President of the United States from an Active Duty Member of the Military," where I compared the oath taken when joining the military to the oath taken when a president is sworn into office. I then talked about the first round of NSA spying revelations (long before Snowden) and the hypocrisy of treating regular Americans as potential enemies by violating the Constitution. This revelation had infuriated me, and I felt like I had to say something publicly.

The letter was published anonymously. I wasn't brave enough yet to be fully public. Rocking the boat was a desire but also a deep, Midwestern fear. And given the limited circulation of the paper and the fact that the readership was already in agreement with the paper's politics I doubt I changed the world or even one person's mind with that one anonymous letter. But I felt like my voice had finally been unleashed.

The letter was also picked up by Tom Barton, a long-time and practically legendary socialist, peace activist, and worker's rights fighter, in his G.I. Special newsletter. Barton's roots went back to the Young People's Socialist League and the protests against the Vietnam War. My writing had become part of that river of idealism.

By the March issue I was ready to write an article and put my name to it. "Why Technology Matters" was a polemic against a bill designed to suppress media technology development, along with the early efforts against net neutrality (before that term was even used) by the telecoms. That article I put my name to, as it was not military-related. This article was my first by-line.

Part of working on the Southern (((i))) was distribution. Independent coffee houses, bars, bookstores, health food stores and the Naro Cinema theater carried the newspaper. It was given away for free, and so piled up with the flyers and free advertisers by the front window. I also would bring a stack with me on base. Dropping a pile surreptitiously on a table in the base laundry facilities, I felt slightly dangerous and rebellious. Whenever I would go back the stack would be gone, probably thrown away by someone. Maybe a few copies had been picked up by sailors. I hoped so, so that they would be introduced to another way of looking at the world.

At times though, the fervent idealism of the anti-war movement could result in a humorlessness and lack of self-deprecation that became uncomfortable. After one newspaper editing session some recreation time at the movies was discussed. One person suggested the Bryan Singer-directed Superman movie that had just come out. But that triggered a diatribe about Superman as a symbol of American Imperialism, etc. etc. My thought was that it's just a movie about a guy who flies around in his underwear and fights crime (though that invites a whole other avenue of over-analysis). With activists, everything becomes a cause, and there's no off switch. Going from the intensity of sea time on the Hawes to the intensity of the anti-war movement, sometimes I just wanted to rest. The summer of 2007 I "rubber-banded" back and forth, wanting a quiet weekend but also wanting to be involved in the movement and push it forward.

Another step in my rebellion was attending a protest for the first time. February 2006 saw a massive protest on a damp and cold day in Washington, D.C., organized by World Can't Wait, a radically left group. Though the official numbers counted only a few thousand protestors, the sight of a snake of humanity encircling the White House was one of the most empowering moments of my life. Walking with those on the wrong side of entrenched political power showed me that rebellion was possible. I discovered that protesting was necessary, and safe. It was as valid a way of participating in the American democracy as voting. And it was patriotic.

Another protest took place in March 2006 against the war, in the vicinity of Fort Bragg in Fayetteville, North Carolina. This was smaller than the D.C. protest of the previous month. This time the weather was sunny and warmer. This protest was more low-key, and included some locals quietly standing in their driveways with American flags. Whether in support or counter-protest, I cannot say. Palumbo asked out loud why this year's protest was thinner and less energetic. I mused that with public opinion against the wars starting to turn perhaps the lower turnout was because we had already done the job and changed the country's attitude. Whether this would result in action by the elected officials remained to be seen.

At the post-march concert was an arc of tables set up by supporting organizations and related causes. One table was selling a full set of underground anti-war newspapers from the Vietnam War, written by and for GIs, the precursor to the Southern (((i))). It made me realize that our little newspaper was part of a larger story. Americans had always spoken to power. Anti-war protesting, the call for peace, went back as far as Thoreau's essay Civil Disobedience. For those of us protesting new wars, the Vietnam-era activists became mentors, passing the torch they kept lit all these decades of complacency. These mentors became important guides and inspirations as the Appeal for Redress project was launched.

The Appeal for Redress

Back in December 2004 I had run into Jon Hutto, the other "old man" from boot camp, at Fair Grounds coffee house in the Ghent district. He was posted in Norfolk with the USS Roosevelt after A-School for journalism. We got caught up and exchanged numbers and agreed to keep in touch between our sea time and deployments. Jon was becoming increasingly politically active. Before joining, he had worked with Amnesty International in the Washington, D.C. area and after boot camp had reconnected with the organization. Through them he started to become involved in the growing movement against the Iraq and Afghanistan wars.

In December of 2005 Jon invited me to a lecture hosted by Amnesty International addressing the intersection of peace movements and military members. Tom Palumbo was hosting and when I had run into Tom earlier he asked me to sit up front and answer questions and provide the perspective of an active duty military member. That night, being in the spotlight and finally having a chance to vocalize my thoughts and feelings to a receptive audience I felt alive again. There were tragedies in the world, in my own world of the military, but I could do something about it. The energy of people power, of a group of citizens banding together to fight injustices inflicted by the powerful on the powerless, made my heart soar. Instead of walking through my military career, zombie-like, suppressing every sense of injustice large and small with cynicism and helplessness, I now knew I could stand up and do something. And not alone. Alone, it's almost impossible to change the world; as part of a movement, we could turn the momentum of war.

Next on the agenda was helping Jon and Amnesty International organize and promote a lecture by David

Cortright in June of 2006. Cortright had written a book, Soldiers in Revolt, that documented the anti-war movement within the military during the Vietnam War. As both an activist and scholar, he recorded the in-service resistance while being in the middle of it. Cortright's book was one of the few to detail this history. Soldiers in Revolt had been reissued to accompany the new wars, since it appeared to many that history was repeating itself. In the movement, we read it for inspiration. An extra chapter for the new edition outlined the beginnings of the in-service resistance against the Iraq and Afghanistan wars that we were part of. Seeing our story in print made the struggle real, and the way our predecessors in Vietnam had helped turn the tide of public opinion promised us the possibility of doing the same and ending our own wars.

Hutto and I reserved space at the South Hampton Roads YMCA and promoted the lecture everywhere we could. We dropped flyers in every coffeehouse and bookshop and anywhere we thought progressive people would see it. Hutto had a good network of activists and friends in the service who he could invite. I had not invited anyone from my ship. Part of this was a desire to keep my private life and my working life separate. Which was strange, since these private activities were meant to directly counter my day job, fighting wars. Another reason was a desire not to get anyone else in trouble. I knew the risk I was taking, being an anti-war activist. Even though I was staying within the letter of regulations, much harm could be done to me informally, or even illegally before my rights were recognized. I did not want to ask anyone else to take the same risk. Most folks I knew in the service were not political and just wanted to get through their enlistment so they could get out and move on with life.

But also, I was just plain afraid. While every sailor complained about the Navy I did not know if that unhappiness would translate into political awareness. For most people, it doesn't. The low voter turnout in every election tells us that. While I'm sure I was known to the authorities, no one on my ship knew about my activities, and I did not know who I could trust with the knowledge. And this semi-anonymity allowed me to go through my workday on the ship quietly. I could do my job, get off duty, then go to my second job: speaking out against the wars.

Looking back, I do regret not saying anything to my shipmates on the Hawes. There were ways to edge towards the subject, evaluate people's opinions without exposing the full story of my anti-war activities upfront. These were interpersonal skills I could have developed but didn't.

The lecture was superb. Every chair was taken, and it became standing room only. Cortright teaches at Norte Dame at the Joan B. Kroc Institute for International Peace Studies. He is a tall, slender and quiet man, very academic, and this lecture was to be one of the first associated with the re-release of Soldiers in Revolt. He kept his lecture short, simple and to the point to leave plenty of time for discussion and questions. Cortright gave us a quick overview of the Vietnam-era GI movement. The sense of continuity struck me. In this room was a man who had been there and fought the same fight against an unjust war that we were fighting. Tom Barton, publisher of GI Special, had come down from New York, bringing with him another moral thread that traced back to the Vietnam War. That night felt like a nexus of ideas and history.

After the lecture, many of us gathered at the house of local Amnesty International members for an active duty-only meeting, with a few close friends and mentors such as Cortright, Barton and Palumbo. The room was packed, with many of us sitting on the floor. Here the conversation became much more radical. Jon was feeling out fellow active duty members for creating some sort of anti-war group within the military itself, along the lines of the movement that Cortright had described to us in his lecture and in the book. The discussion was completely open by design, and nothing was taken off the table. We talked about everything from open protest on base to refusal to deploy to the history of sabotage on ships during the Vietnam War. (I quipped that the Hawes was so old it did a pretty good job sabotaging itself.) I sensed that no one wanted to take the protesting that far, and certainly it wasn't anyone's intention to damage or destroy the ship or flat out disobey orders. But the shock of suggesting actions so radical was important to open the sailors' minds to the realm of possibility, knowing that they could do something about a war they did not support.

David Cortright then told us stories of the retaliations suffered by protesting GIs during Vietnam, both officially and unofficially. His point that ours was a different era with greater consequences was important. Back during the Vietnam War, the idea of anti-war resistance within the military itself was so new and strange that the establishment wasn't sure what to do about it. Certainly, cut-and-dried cases such as going AWOL or sabotage were easy to identify and prosecute. But the ideology was more difficult for the establishment to understand and they never effectively generated a counter-narrative. This time around it would be different. The tools to monitor and disrupt our actions had become more sophisticated and now they knew we would be acting. Some of us, including me and Hutto, had already acted publicly so there was no doubt we were being observed. Post-9/11 the growing anti-Muslim hysteria could try to paint us as secret Al-Qaeda agents (we assuredly were not; we were Americans who cared deeply about our country). And the consequences would be more severe. Even an arrest without a conviction for protesting, "rioting," trespassing, or one of the other vague infractions that authorities use to stop protestors could affect future employment and benefits. After the 1960s, when there was a larger pubic empathy for the counter-culture and the many movements of the time were surrounded by an air of romance, an arrest for protesting years earlier could be blown off with a wink and a nudge and some reminiscing. Not anymore. Our society had become much more rigid and conformist. With the creep of neoliberal economics and culture and now the atmosphere of fear after 9/11 those who stood out in thought, behavior and action could be ostracized very quickly.

So Cortright recommended keeping to the letter of the law and regulations for our own protection. While we still could be attacked through informal channels and methods, the military, being so bound by rules, would not be able to directly punish us if we kept our behavior and speech legal. If they tried, getting legal help was much easier if we obeyed the military's own laws. We could use the inflexible nature of the military against it to protect ourselves as we spoke out.

For most of the rest of the summer of 2006 and into fall the USS Hawes was at sea frequently as the crew trained for a deployment to the Middle East in early 2007. This kept me out of the loop for a while, as when I was in port I mostly wanted to rest. I did attend whatever meetings I could and kept working on the Southern (((i))) here and there. While I was at sea, Hutto kept working and, together with David Cortright and another veteran, Liam Madden, came up with the idea for the Appeal for Redress.

Military law states that service members cannot petition their government directly, because doing so would violate the necessity of obeying orders without question in a military situation. However, service members are still citizens and so may write or speak to their local, state and federal representatives and leaders directly so long as they do so as citizens and not as service members. They can even speak publicly out of uniform and not as representatives of the military. These rights, to speak out as private citizens, were the tools we were going to use to organize.

The Appeal for Redress would take the form of a website, where active duty members would add their names, ranks, and duty status (active or retired) to the Appeal. The wording of the Appeal was:

"As a patriotic American proud to serve the nation in uniform, I respectfully urge my political leaders in Congress to support the prompt withdrawal of all American military forces and bases from Iraq. Staying in Iraq will not work and is not worth the price. It is time for U.S. troops to come home."

The Appeal officially launched in October 2006. While Hutto, Cortright, Madden and others worked at building up the Appeal, I varied between sea time as the USS Hawes worked up to deployment and resting when we were in port. I helped where I could with the Appeal effort and the Southern (((i))), attending meetings and giving input to local actions. I also spent a good amount of time working on a more personal pursuit that was energizing much of my anti-war and anti-militarism sentiments. I was becoming a Buddhist.

I had been introduced to Buddhism long before my Navy days, as an enthusiastic reader of the Beats. Kerouac's "The Dharma Bums" had fired my imagination and I started meditating. While still living at home while attending community college, and later at Western Illinois University, I meditated avidly and read every Buddhist text I could get my hands on. Like most things in the Nebraska phase of my life, what was once my personal core was lost, and my practice faded after some time. I barely used my cushions while living in Lincoln. But being thrust into the harsh military culture reawakened my interest. I felt the need for the inner equanimity, and a worldview that was opposed to the unquestioned violence that we were indoctrinated with daily. Buddhists use the term "Refuge" for their teachings. A refuge was what I needed.

Having the new apartment gave me someplace to set up the cushions, push away the noise and distractions, and meditate once again. Instead of the Zen and Tibetan lineages practiced by my Beat inspirations I meditated in the Theravada school of southeast and southern Asia. The simple basics of Theravada mindfulness, keeping a light and unwavering concentration on the breath, made for a practice that could be pursued solo. Every evening I sat, first for ten minutes, then fifteen, working my way up to thirty or more minutes of meditation per evening. My focus grew stronger, and my body adjusted to the cross-legged posture. As much as possible I maintained that mindfulness away from the cushion, even at work on the ship. Concentrating on drawing a line on a chart, giving it my full attention without distraction, helped carry the calm of the cushion to the ship with me.

This meditation also countered a tendency towards anger. After being abandoned by the girlfriend while in boot camp and thrown in a rootless life without a home or friends, the first two years in the military were a time of depression and fury. I was angry at what happened, and the lack of resources to make things better. I couldn't quit and get a new job. I could not move away. I could not speed up my rise through the ranks to earn more money. Not having the ability to better my circumstances boiled my blood, and it showed. I had gained a reputation for an evil temper on the ship. Those who tend towards anger feel it is empowering, and there is a great sense of justification. Sometimes, there are good reasons to be angry. But after two years the caustic effects were becoming a problem. On almost a daily basis something triggered me and even if there was no external reaction my heart pounded, memories flooded back and I felt no hope for life getting better again.

Moving into my own place and taking up meditation again helped calm those fears and the resulting anger. And being in the anti-war movement was a further antidote to a culture that encouraged anger. I felt empowered in my life again.

After some months of solo meditation, I wanted to practice mindfulness with others. The Norfolk Unitarian Universalist Church had a regular meditation group that I started to attend. This was another connection to civilian life. It was good to be around people who had normal lives. There were people who simply lived. No military, no politics. Regular jobs and families. I was reminded that one day I would return to a simple life as well.

One weekend I snuck out to West Virginia for an Introduction to Meditation retreat at Bhavana Society. My main text for meditation practice was Mindfulness in Plain English, by Bhante Gunaratana. Reading his bio at the back of the book it mentioned that his monastery, Bhavana Society, was in West Virginia. Suddenly realizing that wasn't all that far away, I looked up their website, saw that there was an upcoming beginner's meditation retreat, and promptly signed up.

Unlike civilian jobs, where your weekends off are a given, in the military you are considered on duty 24/7. Therefore, if you want to take a weekend off, you have to spend accumulated leave time for Saturday and Sunday. Suddenly, that generous leave policy doesn't look so great. In addition, you must notify your command if you are going to be more than 50 miles away for any reason. This is in case the ship suddenly has to recall everyone, so from a military standpoint the policy makes sense. But I have never liked explaining myself to authority, considering my off-duty time to be mine, without claim by any person or power. And how to explain a Buddhist meditation retreat to a chief petty officer? So, I just went without telling anyone, seeking no permission and giving no explanation. It was the weekend, and I was not going to see anyone from the ship anyway.

Bhavana Society is a Sri Lankan lineage Theravada monastery, hidden in the peaceful backwoods of West Virginia. I stayed in a kuti, a small raised cabin without electricity. I soaked in the quiet and the green forest, feeling as far away from the military as I could possibly be. Because most of our time was spent in silence, either meditating or listening to dharma talks, I did not have to explain myself to the other retreat attendees. I was afraid of seeing that closed face when you tell someone you are in the military. Without that stigma I felt free.

When you attend a retreat at Bhavana you take the Five Training Precepts. These are temporary monastic vows to abstain from stealing, sexual misconduct, false speech, and intoxication. The very first precept is against the taking of life. The weight of this precept affected me, as it was a direct contradiction to the military "precept" of killing whom I am ordered to kill. While the precept technically would be lifted from me when the retreat was over, I felt the significance of chanting that precept with my own voice, "Pānātipātā veramanī sikkhāpadam samādiyāmi." I did not want to let the precept go after I left. It stayed with me from that moment on.

Ironically, in some ways the retreat felt like being in boot camp. Up at 5 AM, meals taken silently at fixed times, regimented behavior, and so on. I mused to myself that if boot camp had been like this instead of the inane masculine nonsense we had been subjected to, I would have been happy to stay in the military forever.

Into the Public Eye

The morning of January 15, 2007, Martin Luther King Day, I got a call from Hutto, asking me if I would like to be interviewed with him for the Washington Post. I said yes. He asked me to meet him at the MLK monument in Norfolk. There, a reporter interviewed us and a photographer took some photographs of us in front of the monument. Hutto handed me an MLK button. He spoke of being inspired by Dr. King and his anti-war efforts back in the 1960s. When asked about my inspiration, I cited the absurdities of Catch-22 and the insanity of a war based on admitted lies, run poorly due to political dishonesty targeting reality itself and blatant war profiteering (such as the no-bid Halliburton contract).

The same day Hutto and I were interviewed by the Post was the public press conference for the Appeal for Redress, at the same Norfolk Unitarian Church where I had been attending the meditation group. It was an appropriate setting. The anti-war movement of the 1960s, despite images of protesting hippies, had always been powered by religious figures, especially at the beginning. And protesting war was a spiritual action. If one cared only for worldly wealth and success then there was much power and money to be had in war. To embrace the more difficult path, a way of peace, meant turning away from profit, and hate, and the need to dominate. Such a world could still be wealthy, but the easier path has always been through war. Seeing the better way means casting one's eyes up, and growing complete as a person, so that you know that conquering will bring no joy and no immortality, and only the most fleeting of worldly things.

Everyone who was involved with the Appeal was there on stage at the church. At that point there were 1,030 signatures, a significant statement against the war. For the gravity of the occasion I wore a civilian business suit, the first time in who knew how long. Speeches were given, and I was asked to lead the active duty service members in reciting the Appeal for Redress. We also took turns reciting parts of Dr. King's speech "A Time to Break Silence," his seminal anti-war statement given in 1967 at the height of the Vietnam War.

The sections of the speech were handed out randomly, I believe. I was given part two:

> This I believe to be the privilege and the burden of all us who deem ourselves bound by allegiances and loyalties which are broader and deeper than nationalism and which go beyond our nation's self-defined goal and positions. We are called to speak for the weak, for the voiceless, for the victims of our nation and for those it calls "enemy," for no document from human hands can make these humans any less our brothers.

The section was randomly given to me to read, but it seemed as if the force of my anti-war actions, my Buddhist practice, and my observation of the far side of the world I had traveled to were summed up by that short paragraph. It was the perfect piece for me to read to the world.

Afterwards there were more interviews, with the Associated Press, NHK (a television interview in which I could not help looking at the camera, a rookie mistake I regret to this day), and the Virginia Pilot. I suppose being the only person in a suit made interviewers think I was more approachable. Then, I walked away into the dark, going home.

I felt at the center. Everything in the last twelve months of my life, from meeting Tom Palumbo, working on the Southern (((i))), reconnecting with Jon Hutto, the protests, all of those actions led to one singular statement to the world, with other active-duty military members—that the wars were wrong, and they needed to be stopped. It was an American tragedy, a waste of the power and potential and ideals of our country. We were losing American men and women to death and maiming. Thousands of people, not American but our fellow humans nonetheless, were dying from mistakes or sloppiness or being in the wrong place at the wrong time. America was better than this. And those fighting the wars, those who saw the waste and the tragedy in person, had to say something.

Did we stop the wars immediately? No. Changing the direction of an entire country's policy does not happen immediately. There is no romantic hero figure that changes the course of history single-handedly. It makes for good TV and movies but it is never as simple as that. By protesting, by speaking out, by creating and signing the Appeal for Redress we were adding our voices to the many trying to stop the war. Eventually, with enough voices, public opinion turned against the Iraq War and the Afghanistan War. Politicians listened, eventually. Most of the troops came home. Public and journalistic scrutiny made it much more difficult to hide war crimes and waste money and life. The Afghanistan War is not over yet; the Iraq War devolved into a muddle of other crises. But there are many less American troops there, and that has resulted in many less casualties. That is a victory for the anti-war movement. It's only a partial victory. But when trying to stop wars, the struggle never ends. There are always those in power who glory in war and the effort to stop them never ends.

When the reporting came out the next day it was

surreal seeing my picture and name in the Washington Post. Being interviewed for media distributed worldwide, there was no hiding my anti-war feelings and efforts now. I wondered what the reaction would be from my command. We who spoke were within our rights, but would there be some sort of informal retaliation? Would I be called to the captain's cabin for a bitch-out? I knew there were risks involved but I had gone so far at this point without consequence that I discounted the risk.

I walked up the brow of the ship the morning after the presentation nervously. I fully expected to be grabbed or confronted right there on the quarterdeck. I was waved on without comment, to my surprise. Next, I expected to get called aside after morning quarters. Again, nothing. As I went through my workday and nothing happened I realized that most likely no one had even read the article or seen a broadcast. With the readership of newspapers already crashing, and the conservative audience self-ghetto'd into Fox News, an article in the Washington Post might very well go unnoticed among most of the military. The only sign that anyone on the Hawes knew came from a knowing smirk from the executive officer, the ship's second-in-command, who I had always suspected to be a fellow secret progressive from his gentle and quiet manner with the crew.

The public presentation of the Appeal for Redress was my last involvement in the anti-war movement. The next day, the 16th, many of the Appeal for Redress organizers went to Washington to present the Appeal to supportive Congress members on the Capitol steps. I had to go to work on the ship, so I did not go with them. In only a few weeks the USS Hawes would be leaving on another deployment, my second. That would take up most of 2007 and after we returned I would be looking towards my last few months of active duty. I was almost free. I had made my statement to the military, to the country, and to the world. I was ready to move on.

EXIT

Finally, it was time to go. January 11, 2008. Four years of active duty. One last time I drove onto Norfolk Naval Base. I was blasting through my speakers a song by Ted Leo and the Pharmacists, "La Costa Brava," a poignant song about a man waiting to meet a veteran friend on the Mediterranean coast of France. Though no one was waiting for me I felt the same sense of surviving terrible times and wanting to walk away and forget.

On the ship I dashed around, grabbing my service file from the admin office and signing all the requisite paperwork. There were interviews with the command master chief, executive officer and the captain. All knew that they were losing a good sailor, and there's a saying in the military that the good ones never stay. Nothing was going to convince me otherwise, however. I had broken my life when I joined the Navy. Now I could put it back together again.

Many more goodbyes followed throughout the ship, in every division and space. At the quarterdeck an honor guard of sorts of my shipmates in my division gathered to salute me off the ship as I left. As tradition dictated, I was rung off with the ship's bell. Usually this honor is given only to the ship's captain and visiting officers and dignitaries. But on a sailor's last day, enlisted or officer, they are rung off the ship with the same honors. So, the in-port officer of the deck rang two bells of the ship's 1MC, the PA system, and declared "Petty Officer 2nd Class, David Rogers Jr, departing." For the last time, I walked off the USS Hawes.

Leaving the base, I blasted another Ted Leo song. This was his cover of Chumbawamba's "Rappaport's Testament: I Never Gave Up." A brutal and affirming blast of punk, it shouted on my behalf at top volume as I drove through the gate.

And just like that, I was done.

ECHOES OF MEMORY: TEN YEARS LATER

As I write this it is January of 2018. Only a couple of days ago I passed the tenth anniversary of the end of my active duty, the day I said Goodbye to All That. I listened to the same two Teo Leo songs. I was mildly disobedient at work, causing my boss to wryly comment on my inherent rule-breaking. After ten years, my attitude towards authority (not going to listen much) and duty (always do your duty, but you decide what that duty is) has not changed one bit.

One month after my discharge from active duty I got a job doing Geographic Information Systems work for a small start-up company. These were my first civilian co-workers in four years. Some of them became good friends, and their friendship helped the process of becoming a civilian again. I found that I went back to civilian life easily. My inherent resistance to the authoritarianism of the military had kept a small part of me safe, a seed of self that bloomed quickly when the uniform came off.

Another step in my journey to civilian life was becoming a regular meditator at Wat Pasantidhamma in Carrolton, Virginia. I was introduced to the Buddhist temple by a Thai friend of mine. Immediately, I felt at home. Wednesday nights were "American night," where the monks would instruct and facilitate discussions in English, helped by a friendly Thai member of the sangha. The group of regular Wednesday night attendees became close to me and I felt that I had a real community of friends once again. My practice deepened, and I came to openly refer to myself as a Buddhist.

The temple community also provided my first dating experiences after the Navy. The entire time I was in the military I had no relationships. I tried, but the stigma of the uniform was impossible to overcome. I faced an assumption that I was just like all the other sailors, ravenously hormonal and that I just wanted to use a girl and then abandon her, knocked up and neglected. This was not my personality and never has been or will be. But that was the perception and I could not get anyone to see "me" behind the uniform. Being able to interact with women again without the military coming between us made me feel human again.

But being a civilian also brought me into contact with some atavistic attitudes that surprised me. In the Navy I had (ironically) avoided most of the conservative military culture, by being part of the anti-war movement and surrounding myself with progressives and thinkers and meditators. Now, thrown into civilian life in the Tidewater region of Virginia, I came across a fervently racist form of conservatism that I was dismayed to find still existed.

Fall 2008 saw the election of Barack Obama to President of the United States. In the months leading up to the election, as it became more apparent that he was going to win, the entirely white male management of the company I worked for let it be known that it was apparent to them who among the employees was going to vote Democrat, and that we should keep in mind that Virginia was a right-to-work state. The threat was obvious (and completely misunderstood what "right-to-work" means; we were not union and didn't pay union dues). The company had just hired a professional human resources manager, so the issue was brought up to her. Management backed off but given that the same management consisted of the company's founders and their high school friends, there was no doubt that the political climate in the office would not change.

Eventually, the company went under, as many start-ups do. It was my second lay-off. We had been told that there was a big contract and our jobs were safe for a long time but, at the meeting where everyone got laid off, the company president admitted that was a lie and there was no contract. After being attacked for the supposed immorality of voting Democrat, the management's demanded morality of personal, political and corporate loyalty proved hypocritical.

The company closed doors in January 2009, right when the Great Recession hit. Their failure was unrelated to the Recession, being entirely self-inflicted, but it put us in the unemployment line. I spent the next six months at Wat Pasantidhamma most days, assisting the monks, meditating, and enjoying the quiet bliss. Eventually I got a new job at Joint Task Force-Civil Support and, in a sense, partly re-entered the military.

JTF-CS is a small joint military command meant to assist in disasters, large-scale terrorist attacks in particular, within the United States using active-duty, regular military assets. The unit deployed for exercises a couple times of year. Sometimes you got to stay in a hotel. Often it was a barracks on a military base. I worked in the command center creating and displaying maps. As a civilian contractor I wasn't subject to most of the military nonsense but sometimes I wondered why I had not fallen farther from the tree. My justification at the time was that in the middle of the Great Recession beggars could not be choosers, and it paid well enough to replenish my savings after six months of unemployment. Still, it seemed that as long as I stayed in Virginia I would not be able to get away from the military. I resolved myself even more firmly to move on. I dumped all my military history books on the break room table one day with a sign saying, "Free for the taking." I started to research graduate school, so I could apply my GIS skills to something non-violent and constructive to human society.

JTF-CS was deployed to Fort Lewis, Washington, to cover the Winter Olympics in Vancouver in 2010. For three weeks we sat there on standby in case there was a terrorist attack on the Olympics. Keeping JTF-CS deployed for three weeks was expensive, and rumor had it that the chain of command was grumbling about the costs. Those costs had to be justified and JTF-CS being a contingency plan, deployed just in case something unlikely happened, it was a difficult justification. Someone, in a meeting, came up with the idea of raising the threat level on the protestors. The Olympics had seen some mild protesting by First Nations and cost-of-housing activists, barely disruptive and certainly not terrorism. But if we raised our threat level assessment on these groups, well, it might help justify our high deployment costs. The fact that this was a lie and the protestors in question were not even American citizens, and were protesting Canadian domestic issues without violence, didn't seem to faze anyone. The democratic actions of civilians in another country were useful to brand as "potential threats" if it kept the money flowing.

I decided while on that deployment that I had had enough. I would leave Virginia and any involvement with the military life, no matter how valuable my security clearance was or how easy it was to get a contractor job. I was noticing a creeping authoritarianism in our country. Sometimes it was blatant, such as threatening left-leaning employees for their voting choices. Or it was a simple desire to keep that military and homeland security budget expanding, so why not exaggerate a threat? The fear after 9/11 had not gone away and it was a useful tool. Some used it for their own agenda. For others it was simply a convenient lever. I refused to contribute to that machine any longer.

In 2010 the USS Hawes was decommissioned and towed to the ghost fleet for storage up the James River. My father, who always keeps an eye on Navy news, told me about the decommissioning. I felt nothing, not fondness or poignancy or even scorn. I wasn't looking back for any reason. The military period of my life was done.

I left Virginia for Denver in 2011 and earned a graduate degree in environmental policy at University of Denver. It was the journey I should have taken from Nebraska in 2004, instead of joining the military.

On my long drive between Virginia and Colorado I stopped home in the Chicago area to stay with my parents for a few days and to see a friend, someone who had been my best friend since we met in middle school. Over many beers we got to talking about politics and the state of the world. After a while, the conversation became unreal.

First, my friend tried to tell me about how racist President Obama was, while himself using a severe racial epithet to refer to the President. Then, after I described my time at Bhavana Society, I was told that I was a betrayer to my race, since Christianity was the only proper religion for white people. He tried to tell me that socialism was fascist. Voting had to be limited to only a select few, because if everyone could vote then they would vote to take all the money from rich people. And lastly (though I'm sure there's plenty I forgot) he described how important it was that Germany invade Poland immediately, in order to defend itself from Russia. When I pointed out that there's this thing called NATO just for that reason and that both countries are already members, I was told that I just don't understand, and got a long description of the history of the Teutonic Knights.

The sheer bizarreness of his beliefs took me aback. I knew he had a conservative bent but that had given way to sheer insanity. Delusions, false equivalencies, and historical fantasies dominated his world view. I asked myself, if I had met him now, would I even be friends with him? The answer was no. I could not be friends with someone who was so hostile to not only my own beliefs, as his attack on my Buddhism stung the most, but also basic concepts of freedom, democracy and decency to others not like ourselves.

It also was, though I did not know it at the time, a preview of the alt-right. Here, five years before the election of 2016, all the paranoid delusions and hate that a future America would face were on display, a poison flowing through our country that no one could see yet. I wish I had paid more attention but at the time it all seemed so outlandish. Any attempt to argue or counter-explain was quickly steamrollered as he moved on to the next bizarre "fact" without pause, making any attempt to inject some sanity and truth into this rant impossible. It was sad to see many of the elements of anti-democratic, anti-peace philosophy in a good friend, and spun together into a delusional froth. I lost a friend to paranoia and hate.

As for myself, I now have the life I wanted and was not brave enough to embrace so long ago. I have been using my GIS skills for electric utility design and not the military or homeland security. I hike the wilds and explore the art and music of the city. I finally am living a life that resembles the one I have always imagined for myself.

Yet, the military still lingers in the fabric of my life. News from the areas I served still affects me, such as the boat refugees in the Mediterranean and the Gulf of Yemen. I can see them clearly in my mind's eye when I read the news: the dirty boats, the wounds and the suffering. The on-and-off threat of war with Iran, in particular the threats against shipping in the Strait of Hormuz, puts me back on deck, navigating furiously to keep the USS Hawes in lane, and the tension of communicating with the Iranian Navy to declare our intentions to run the Strait in accordance with the freedom of navigation laws. By the way, the regular Iranian Navy was actually quite nice on the radio, not like the Revolutionary Guard at all. There are factions and subtleties within other nations, even enemy nations, that we should keep in mind when news reports try to simplify the story into stark good and bad, black and white.

With other veterans, even those on the conservative side, I exchange war stories and a shared experience. There's still a sense of duty, the desire to get done what must be done no matter what. That never leaves a veteran. I run into few sailors but Army and Marine veterans are relatively common, and everyone has a story to tell. Sometimes it's a funny one, often the stories are haunting, or simply hinted at. PTSD is everywhere, if you know how to listen.

Even though the Iraq and Afghanistan wars were the wars of the Millennial generation, it seems that the memory of the conflict has already faded. Perhaps this is because so few served (no more than 1% of the U.S. population is active duty military at any time), or because like the decade after Vietnam, many Americans are trying to forget.

Even more obscure to most Americans is the history of the anti-war movement, and the GI anti-war movement in particular. After I grumbled about the use of the term "Winter Soldier" for a Marvel Universe movie title, a co-worker who is well-versed in nerd knowledge informed me that the Winter Soldier wasn't whatever I was talking about, but actually Bucky, Captain America's sidekick turned Soviet supervillain. My grumble turned into an attempt to educate him about the Vietnam Veterans Against the War (VVAW) "Winter Soldier" hearings in 1971 and the Thomas Paine origination of the term ("The summer soldier and the sunshine patriot will, in the crisis, shrink from services of their country; but he that stands it now deserves the love and thanks of man and woman."). The co-worker's attention wandered, and he steered the conversation back to more nerd knowledge, where he could feel superior again. The lack of interest in the struggle against war by GIs, or even the basic texts of American history, was disappointing but not surprising. So much is being lost to the daily conveyor of trivial information. No one's feet stand on the bedrock of America anymore.

*

Why peace? Why, in a world that seems steeped in violence, try to stop war? Why bother?

War, to Generation X, did not seem possible for most of our childhood. As an American kid in the 1970s, you learned about World War Two, America's finest moment, the Good War. Vietnam, our recent shame, was not re-enacted. No kid played "Cold War." What would that be anyway? Pretending to sit in a bunker staring at a big red button that says "Nuke" on it?

The Good War and the Bad War, World War Two and Vietnam. Triumph and shame. Both were there in the American psyche, influencing a young American boy's mind safely.

Safely, because they were oh so distant. The mythology of World War Two said that America could fight for what is good, and war is good. The mythology of Vietnam said that America could be evil and wrong, and that war is wrong.

The Cold War told us that war is too terrible to contemplate, so war was impossible. Playing at war as a kid was a historical anachronism, so don't worry about it. History was over, America won, and the country would never be at war again.

It was safe to play at war, even though (or because) some would say that violence is humanity's natural state. I disagree. On a daily basis, most folks are not violent.

While reading this book you are most likely not engaging in warfare. Instead, you are peacefully sitting in a chair (and I hope drinking something smoothly alcoholic). Every day billions of humans go about their lives and don't kill anyone. Most people live their entire lives without ever ending another human's life. To cynically claim that humanity is inherently violent and so wars must be waged is disingenuous. The evidence for our peaceful nature is all around us.

Certainly, everyone has a capacity for violence. Anyone will defend themselves when attacked. Carnivores and omnivores must commit violence to eat, even though most of us don't do so directly anymore. Plenty of people get angry every day. But that violence is personal. Regular people are not taking that anger and organizing it for political ends. Personal violence ends with the law, or self-control, or forgiveness.

The organized and political violence that we call war is not a product of human nature. It is the creation of a few who crave power over all others. To make us kill for their interests means convincing us it is in our interest to do so. It means convincing us that wars desired by politicians, the powerful and the wealthy, is necessary to our personal survival, our happiness, our sense of self and ultimately, ironically, our own peacefulness. Go to war, we are told, and we will be better men and women and real Americans.

There are some ways we can counter this narrative, first for oneself and then for the nation. First ask yourself, when told that the military is a good career for you by a recruiter, "What will I miss? Where will my friends be? How often will I see my family? What else can I do that allows me to stay in my life now, and get the 'benefits' I'm being sold on?" There are so many other ways to live besides the military life.

Remember, since you are technically on duty 24/7,

your average wage in the military at the beginning is well below minimum wage. You'd be better off flipping burgers. And you would get to sleep in your own bed every night. Flipping burgers instead of being in the military means you have the time to figure out what else to do with your life. While on military deployment to the other side of the world, your options to explore your options are highly limited.

Imagine injury. Life without limbs. Not being able to walk. Paralyzed. Or blind, deaf, or both. How difficult would everyday tasks become? How would you make a living? How would you live? Do you think the Veteran's Administration will take care of you? You already know the headlines about how dysfunctional that organization is. Congress loves to make war while avoiding all responsibility for the consequences. Those are all yours to deal with for the rest of your life, alone.

Now picture death. Yours. Terror as you bleed uncontrollably, knowing you only have moments left before you lose consciousness. Looking down at your body and seeing pieces missing. Or a death so sudden you are simply gone, no chance to react, no chance to say goodbye. Less than silence, less than darkness. Just the unknowable nothingness on the other side of death.

Got all that? Now imagine someone your age on the other side, an Iranian, a Russian, a North Korean, thinking all the same thoughts you just did. Who do you have more in common with? Him, or the powerful people in both countries trying to get you to kill one another?

That's the personal loss, individual. American society also loses from war. Imagine a national budget given entirely to war. Can you picture a country without national parks? Imagine everyone's old age without Medicare. Does everyone have the resources to take care of their retired parents? Can we individually save enough to take care of ourselves when the GDP is drained for war? How would that drag down everyone's personal finances? And how heavy would the waste of war weigh on the economy?

Picture everyone of draft age gone, sent away to fight. What will happen to universities? What will become of businesses that cater to new college graduates, new homeowners, new parents? If the young are not here to start their adult lives, they cannot contribute ideas, energy, and idealism to the nation.

If our country spent even less on infrastructure than we do now, what would the highways look like? How congested would our airports be? If, as some anti-government economists suggested, every road was converted into a toll road instead of spending tax money on maintenance, how terrible would the gridlock be?

Much of this is not speculation, just an extension of what is true now. The tax burden of the military is already limiting the non-war functions of our society. Half of your Federal taxes goes to the Department of Defense. If we can get back even a good fraction of that, there would be no worry about Social Security, underfunded National Parks, or the national debt. Or if you like, imagine the tax cut we could all have if we spent less on war. The cost of war hurts all of us, liberal and conservative alike. Ending our wars benefits all of us, Americans of every political tribe. Money "invested" in war gives us no return. War makes nothing new. War destroys everything it touches. The money is wasted and doesn't bring a tide that could lift all boats.

Through this lens, our conflicts in Yemen, Somalia, Iraq, Syria, Afghanistan, and deployments in countries around the world that no American has heard of (and our legislators don't even know about) all fail the needs of our country. None of these wars make American lives better or more peaceful. They have the opposite effect of dedicating everyday Americans to economic, political and personal misery. Our wars are a threat to ourselves.

Not coincidentally, those who urge us to kill for our country in this era of American politics rarely have served themselves. They were too scared or too important to join the military. Now, they wish to demonstrate their importance and power by ordering others to do what they would not. They avoid the consequences, they never saw the destruction, and so they never learn to value the peace. War makes them powerful, at everyone else's expense. War is just another expression of selfishness for these men.

There are many reasons for the American penchant for war. Putting aside history as just a series of symptoms, the core reason, I believe, is the idea and structure of American masculinity. Our presented ideal is that a real American man is always ready for violence, dominates those around him, hates anyone different, pollutes the earth, and feels neither empathy nor guilt. War is waged against the world through pollution and destructive extraction. War is waged against minorities by denying them the right to vote and militarizing the police presence in their communities. War is waged against workers by stagnating their wages and preventing the formation of unions. There are countless more examples of the masculine ideological warfare fought every day. And in every instance, the side that is presented as manly is the side waging the warfare on the weak. The workers, the minorities and the planet itself are disparaged as unworthy, feminine. If they resist and fight back against the injustices being inflicted upon them it's not a display of their own strength—it's whining. The right thing for a man to do is associate himself with the powerful, not the weak, and strive for power himself.

One time on Facebook, a friend reposted a comment from a retired military officer. The officer snidely joked that all the girlfriends of anti-war protesters must be disappointed in their men, and they should go for the "real" men who fight the wars they are protesting. As someone who did both, I found the assumption bemusing. Between war and anti-war, the latter took far more bravery. Why? Fighting a war is frightening, but you have all the might of the most powerful military in history on your side. If any of the pirates or Iranian Revolutionary Guard had attacked us, the chances of defeat for the USS Hawes was zero. If things got bad, we could call in air support or other ships. Victory was all but assured, even if we suffered losses. But standing up, walking in protest, saying publicly to the powerful, "No, you are wrong"? That was much more frightening. All the political and economic establishment is against you at that point; your survival depends on a thin veneer of law and the hope that shame will stay the hand of power.

After our boarding team returned from helping the Somali refugee boats, the USS Hawes rumor mill quickly reported that some of our VBSS team members returned in tears at seeing the plight of the refugees. Naturally, they were ridiculed by some for being "pussies," and displaying an emotional reaction to human suffering. But what other reaction can a person have? The refugees were not enemies, just people in need. The help we could give was limited, and frustratingly so. The only humane reaction is empathy, sadness, and being brave enough to openly display those emotions. Who were the real men? Those crying, or those doing the ridiculing? Because, of course, the ones doing the disparaging were safely on the ship and had never volunteered to be on the VBSS team. It's easy to criticize someone else's bravery, both physical and emotional, from a place of cowardice.

In 1914, on the Western Front of World War One, a miracle happened. In the "Christmas Truce," soldiers on both sides declared their own end to hostilities without permission from their leaders. They got out of their trenches, talked, exchanged food, cooked, played soccer, sang carols, and acted like humans. They knew they had no reason to be there. It was a great moment for humanity, for peace, and for masculinity. They found another way.

Of course, the leaders and commentators were incensed. How dare these common men not hate each other when ordered to do so? Didn't they understand the big picture? Were they not patriots? Did they not love their country? What traitors. No, they did not understand the big picture because the big picture never understood them. They only cared about the small picture: hearth, home, family, friends. Life. The level of life at which most of us live our lives, and the level we need to defend against those who want us to sacrifice ourselves for their "big picture."

If warfare is an unnatural state of humanity, and American masculinity is the driver of American warfare, then traditional American masculinity itself is unnatural. To end American wars a new way of being a man must be developed, a way that creates and protects and respects, and does not destroy.

Peace means daily life simply happens. People wake up, go to work, come home, make a living, see their families, play with their children, love their spouses, support their parents, read a good book, watch some TV, cook delicious food, laugh with their friends, travel, wonder at the world, make love, drink with joy, and live life. Peace is the act of simply living, the natural state of humanity.

War disrupts and end all these things. No content person wants to go to war. No one wants to leave the good things in life behind, either in the temporary separation of enlistment and deployment or the permanent separation of the grave. War is unnatural to the human condition. It is imposed on us by a few powers, a handful of leaders who want the common people to kill strangers, to the profit of the few and the detriment of the many.

War leads to dissolution of both the society and the individual. Peace means letting everyone live their lives, from start to end. I want peace. I want to live my life the way I want from start to end, and see that everyone else does as well. I want to create things, not destroy them. A masculinity that is based on destroying life instead of letting it be is no way to be a man.

Further Reading

Cortright, David. *Soldiers in Revolt: GI Resistance During the Vietnam War.* (2nd Ed.) Haymarket Books, Chicago: 2005.

Hansen, Louis. "On Day Honoring Pacifist, Troops Join in Dissent of War." *The Virginia-Pilot,* January 16, 2007.

Hutto Sr., Jonathan W. *Anti-war Soldier.* Nation Books, NY: 2008.

Weeks, Linton. "Why they Fight—From Within." *Washington Post,* January 16, 2007.

About Atmosphere Press

Atmosphere Press is an independent, full-service publisher for excellent books in all genres and for all audiences. Learn more about what we do at atmospherepress.com.

We encourage you to check out some of Atmosphere's latest nonfiction releases, which are available at Amazon.com and via order from your local bookstore:

Rags to Rags, nonfiction by Ellie Guzman
The Naked Truth, nonfiction by Harry Trotter
Heat in the Vegas Night, nonfiction by Jerry Reedy
Evelio's Garden, nonfiction by Sandra Shaw Homer
Difficulty Swallowing, essays by Kym Cunningham
A User Guide to the Unconscious Mind, nonfiction by Tatiana Lukyanova
To the Next Step: Your Guide from High School and College to The Real World, nonfiction by Kyle Grappone
Breathing New Life: Finding Happiness after Tragedy, nonfiction by Bunny Leach
Channel: How to be a Clear Channel for Inspiration by Listening, Enjoying, and Trusting Your Intuition, nonfiction by Jessica Ang
Love Your Vibe: Using the Power of Sound to Take Command of Your Life, nonfiction by Matt Omo
Leaving the Ladder: An Ex-Corporate Girl's Guide from the Rat Race to Fulfilment, nonfiction by Lynda Bayada
Letting Nicki Go: A Mother's Journey through Her Daughter's Cancer, nonfiction by Bunny Leach

About the Author

David Rogers Jr. started his professional writing career with a second place in the Heroes' Voices National Veterans Poetry Contest. He has published further poetry in *Metonym Journal* and for the San Antonio Water System. Most recently, a creative non-fiction essay appeared in *Fossil News: The Journal of Avocational Paleontology*. He lives outside Denver, Colorado.

CPSIA information can be obtained
at www.ICGtesting.com
Printed in the USA
LVHW091012020220
645569LV00003B/767

9 781646 693481